MOSES
WAS A
BASKET CASE

Hilarious true stories to encourage and inspire

J.J.JASPER

BrettMorgan Publishing

To my friend
Edith
God Bless
Prov 3:5,6

Moses was a Basket Case
Copyright © 2001 James A. Jasper

Published by BrettMorgan Publishing

Packaged by Pine Hill Graphics

Cover design by Brad Bullock

Publisher's Cataloging-in-Publication
(Provided by Quality Books, Inc.)

Jasper, J.J.
    Moses was a basketcase : hilarious true stories to
    encourage and inspire / J.J. Jasper. -- 1st ed.
        p. cm.
        ISBN 0-9714103-4-8

    1. Christian life--Anecdotes. 2. Family--Religious
    aspects--Christianity--Anecdotes. I. Title.

BV4517.J37 2001   248.4'02'07
                         QBI01-701307

Printed in the United States of America.

DEDICATION
With love and gratitude to the One who makes life worth living and to my precious girls, Melanie, Lauren and Sadie Morgan.

Acknowledgments

I owe much gratitude to many people. I am grateful to my parents, Alvah and Martha Jasper, for their love and support. Thanks to Dr. Donald E. Wildmon and American Family Radio, friends, family, co-workers and in-laws. My wife Melanie typed and proofed for hours on end – thank you. Special thanks to Randall Murphree, Ed Vitagliano and Rusty Benson for editing and encouragement. Last but not least, without the constant prodding of my dear friend Allen Wildmon, this project would never have seen the light of day.

TABLE OF
CONTENTS

Preface

Introduction

1 *Growing Up* 9

2 *Chifforobe* 19

3 *The Dump Truck* 25

4 *First Flight* 31

5 *Radio and Music* 39

6 *Practical Jokes* 47

7 *Cotton-Pickin' Chicken Chunker* 57

8 *My Girls* 63

9 *Bed and Breakfast* 77

10 *Humor* 83

11 *Mistletoe* 93

12 *Lauren* 103

13 *Hope* 115

14 *The Shack* 125

PREFACE

Rick Robertson is a brilliant radio copywriter, co-worker and trusted friend. He has been a source of encouragement for many years. Everyone who knows Rick testifies of his incredible love for God and his devotion to his precious family. Rick also has a wry sense of humor. I had finished the first chapter of this book and asked Rick to please critique it for me. Hoping for his approval as he finished reading, I explained how I wanted the book to inspire and encourage. I hoped it would be interesting and be a blessing. When he finished the last sentence and looked up I asked him point blank, "Rick do you think people are going to get their money's worth?"

After an extended pause, he finally said, "You'd better put some coupons in the back of the book!" Well I don't want to spoil the surprise, but you have my permission right now to look in the back of this book and see how I occasionally accept wise counsel even if it's administered with a twinkling eye. It is my desire that you enjoy this book and I *do* hope you are entertained, encouraged, inspired and receive some value from our time together even if it's only a chuckle or a grin, because laughter is the best medicine.

INTRODUCTION

For years I've said the most exciting thing in my life was finding a cologne that makes me irresistible to women...it smells like Wal-Mart!

Having the opportunity to write this book is exciting. What a privilege to share some personal experiences and thoughts to help you laugh and provide encouragement. Perhaps you purchased this book or received it as a gift, for whatever reason you are reading this...thank you.

Do you know how you can dream about something for so long and so vividly that when you arrive it seems like you've already been there? Like a young bride who has rehearsed her wedding day so many times in her mind's eye, I always felt I would one day be an author. Writing this book is a dream come true. This is an honor, a privilege and an answered prayer.

I wrote this book for three reasons:

➤ To make you laugh.
➤ Encourage and inspire you.
➤ To earn some diaper money!

Part of the proceeds from the sale of these books will go to feed hungry children...two immediately come to mind.

Also scripture teaches we should do all that we do to glorify God and it's my humble prayer that in someway, somehow He will be honored with this project.

And whatever you do, whether in word or deed, do it all in the name of the Lord Jesus, giving thanks to God the Father through Him. (Colossians 3:17)

1

GROWING UP

I eat breakfast with a half-million people each week-day morning. This is possible because I am the morning on-air personality for the American Family Radio network, which consists of approximately 200 radio stations in 34 states. AFR is also broadcast live via the internet.

My job is to help wake America up on the right side of the bed with a hearty, "Good morning, time to get up, you can do it, c'mon it's time to rise and shine!" I try to offer a balanced combination of great Christian music interspersed with Bible verses, quips, quotes, humorous stories and one-liners. Some say I have the gift of gab. I think I have a big mouth.

This much is true, however – I love the Lord. I love people and enjoy a rewarding career that consists of getting to love and encourage folks for a living. God has truly given me an incredible opportunity. I am blessed with more than I deserve and I am very grateful.

My real name is James Alvah Jasper. During my sopho-more year in high school, I worked part-time in a shoe store. Judy Morton, a co-worker noticed a resemblance between my personality and that of the then popular tele-vision comedian J. J. Walker – otherwise known as "Kid

Dyn-o-mite." The two J's from James Jasper had already garnered an occasional J. J. connection to J. J. Walker, but Judy branded me with the "J. J." Jasper moniker, and the nickname stuck.

I was born and raised in Owensboro, Kentucky. If this book turns out okay, we can thank the Lord, if it doesn't... well, I was born and raised in Kentucky! Maybe an illustration will explain my point. There was an ol' Kentucky boy from the hills who was in his pickup truck coming down an exit ramp that merged with a major highway. He was wearing bib overalls and the truck was quite a sight. The paint was faded, the fender was flapping and the old truck was smoking. Maybe you've seen someone like this in your neck of the woods. There was a yield sign at the bottom of the exit ramp. The old fella reached the yield sign and never even slowed down. He drove right past the sign, a car hit him and they skidded to a halt on the side of the highway.

The city slicker in the car jumped out and was livid. "You stupid hick! Didn't you see that yield sign?" he shouted.

To which the Kentucky boy replied, "Yeah, and I yield at ya three times to look out!"

On a sad note a man went to the doctor and was told he only had six months to live. His knees buckled, he sat down, regained his composure and asked the doctor, "Only six months to live? What should I do?"

The doctor said, "Move to Kentucky, marry a widow with ten kids and start raising hogs."

The man was dumbfounded, repeated the prescription then asked, "Will that make me live longer?"

The doctor said, "No, but those six months will seem like a lifetime!"

Actually, I am very proud to claim Kentucky as my home state. I hope the Bluegrass State feels likewise and claims me as a native son.

Someone once said a speaker has to earn the right to be heard. My guess is that this goes for an author as well. I wasn't planning to get this personal, this early in the book, but there are some things about me I guess you should know.

When I was born, I couldn't walk – the doctors said it would be about a year. I was born without teeth, had no hair when I was born and my elbow was halfway up my arm. Oh, there's more. I was born right here in the United States and when I was born I couldn't speak English! Not a word of it! Not only that but my whole body was covered with epidermis. And I might as well be the one to tell you – lest you read about it in a tabloid – I was born naked!

Okay, okay, I admit it's difficult for me to remain serious for very long. But this zany, off-the-wall, wacky sense of humor has served me well in youth ministry for many years, and lends a helping hand for early morning radio.

Seriously, we lived in the east end housing projects when I was born. It was undoubtedly, the roughest crime-ridden area in our fair city. After several moves, we "arrived" when we moved to Ridgewood Street. Davy Roberts, my boyhood best friend used to tell his mom that everybody should have been lucky enough to grow up on Ridgewood! There were 21 boys on our short dead-end street. Twenty-one boys – can you imagine? Just by being a dead-end street, Ridgewood provided familiarity and fraternity. Every yard was the same size. Identical houses in cookie cutter fashion stood in neat little rows. The only differences were the colors. It was post war architecture at its finest.

Because of the number of boys on our street it was a

sandlot dream come true. We played every sport in every kind of weather. Anytime of day you could find us in someone's backyard pretending to be Joe Namath, Johnny Bench or any number of our sports heroes. I wouldn't take any amount of money for the endless hours of full contact, no holds barred football (or full contact wiffle ball for that matter) that we enjoyed. We played in the mud, pouring rain and snow.

We actually produced many all-state and all-American athletes from our street. Several coaches from our local high school would notice someone excelling in sports and ask, "You wouldn't happen to be from Ridgewood, would you?" We took the phrase "boys of summer" to a new level. We squeezed every single drop out of every single summer.

There was a wholesale effort by all the families on the street to get us all raised and keep us from incarceration. You were fair game to anyone's mom or dad. There was an unwritten rule that any parent could discipline anybody's kid. Everyone looked out for each other.

The neighborhood was like one big family. For example, Clifton and Geneva Roberts' house was the unofficial home base for Ridgewood. Clifton was a coach-like surrogate father for us boys and a great role model. He was a *big* man, inside and out. Geneva was like the den mother of our street. More often than not, their backyard served as the hangout for us all. One couple, Merimee and Virgie Clark, removed the cars from their garage, filled it full of weights and turned it into a gym for us boys. The gesture was nicer than you realize – considering they had no children our age! There was an uncanny unity on Ridgewood.

There was a large field behind our street where we did it all. We built a regulation size baseball diamond complete with a backstop fence. Later, we fenced it in, built stables and raised horses. Having ponies and horses to ride satisfied all of our cowboy fantasies, and we had our own amateur rodeos that were wild, wooly and unplugged. Later we traded the horses for motorcycles. We turned the field into a make shift motor-cross track. When one person did something, everyone else followed suit. Yes, we did it all in that field of dreams.

There was a camaraderie among us guys that I really can't quite put into words. We were all close in age, we grew up together. We lost teeth together, got black eyes together and played sports together. We all got our driver's licenses and started dating at nearly the same time. For sure, there was a fierce competition in all we did, but we had a "Semper Fi" loyalty to one another. You see, we shared hopes, dreams, laughs and tears – together. Some of the strongest bonds and greatest memories of my life trace their roots to Ridgewood. It doesn't take much, a familiar sound, a certain smell – I'm transported back to those good ol' days with my brother Mike, Larry, Bulldog, Ronnie Joe, Denny, Ronnie Dale, Davy, the Beards, the Quinns and the rest of the Ridgewood gang. I think Davy was right: everybody should have been lucky enough to grow up on Ridgewood.

Our family was Southern Baptist. My parents were hardworking, wonderful people, who loved us and taught us right from wrong. We weren't raised in a model Christian home, per se. I'm thankful for seeds of the gospel that were planted by many different people in my formative years. When I was approximately 12 years old, I "walked the aisle" and as best as I knew how, made a commitment to Christ. Whether there was lack of discipline or lack of discipleship, I quickly returned to my old way of living and some would even argue that my conversion "didn't take."

Actually, I was not a bad kid growing up. I was a good

student, a paperboy, a fair athlete and a student council officer. I was among the last of my friends to start smoking and drinking. However, during my senior year I caved in to peer pressure, chose the wrong friends and made many terrible decisions. Because I lacked a solid relationship with Jesus Christ and I longed for acceptance and popularity, my partying intensified. Before long – with my poor choices of abusing alcohol and marijuana and making wrong decisions on dates – my life quickly careened out of control. College plans were derailed and I was rudderless, drifting with no other ambition except to get high and have fun.

I moved in with my godly grandmother. At the lowest point in my life (I'm leaving out a lot of unpleasant details), my grandmother's prayers and my uncle's boldness to share his faith got my attention. My uncle, Paul Gatewood, was a very religious person and very active in his church. Although he was the most *religious* person I knew, by his own admission something vital was missing in his life. Then something happened. He experienced a radical salvation encounter with Jesus Christ. He described it as being "born again" as explained in the third chapter of John, in the Bible. He explained clearly that there was a difference between being "religious" and having a genuine personal relationship with the living Lord Jesus.

I wondered if he had gone off the deep end. He scared me and made me uncomfortable with all that spiritual talk. Sometimes the fear would turn to anger. But he persisted with prayer and remained a bold witness for Christ. I watched my uncle's life closely for over a year. He was a changed man – for the better.

But while his life was marked with a peace and a purpose, mine continued to spiral downward. While my uncle's life was getting much better, and I saw lots of improvement, mine was unraveling, and I hit bottom. I was drinking and smoking pot everyday. I had lost my girlfriend, lost my job and totaled my car. I weighed less than 120 lbs and had completely lost hope. At one point I even considered suicide.

My grandmother's prayers and my uncle's willingness to declare God's love paid off. On bended knee in the wee hours of a winter's morning in January 1977, I realized my need for God, humbled myself, asked God to forgive me and received Jesus Christ into my heart and life by faith. It worked. He forgave me according to His word. Jesus Christ *is* a life changer! I haven't touched drugs, drunk a drop of alcohol or smoked a cigarette since January 15, 1977. I have lots of room for improvement, but to God be the glory for doing a supernatural work in my life that brought miraculous changes. "For by grace are ye saved through faith; and that not of yourselves; *it is* the gift of God: not of works lest any man should boast," (Ephesians 2: 8-9 KJV).

Today, I am happily married with two beautiful healthy children and I am enjoying a life that seems more like a fairy tale. Everyday living life for me is a dream come true. Every bit of success I enjoy hinges on that decision I made to surrender my life to the Lord Jesus Christ. He has given *me* a life of peace and purpose. There is no greater joy than to know your sins are forgiven and you are in right relationship with your Maker. Things have been going so well for so long now that I sometimes want to pinch myself to see if it's true. I feel like a boy Cinderella, and it's all because of Jesus. He was born of a virgin, lived a sinless life, died on a cross for our sins and on the third day He rose again. You ask me how I know He lives, He lives within my heart!

These days life is good. When I'm not on the radio

spending weekday mornings with listeners – who seem more like family than anything else – I'm traveling on frequent speaking and stand-up comedy engagements. As a family, we love to travel, and are blessed to be able to do that together.

We enjoy involvement and activities in our local church. Some of our favorite leisure activities include hanging out with friends, camping and motorcycle riding. We enjoy all sports. We are an avid outdoors family and relish time spent fishing and boating. We live in a lakeside cabin that we built ourselves. We are thankful for the wonderful exciting life God has given us.

Throughout my life, I've been accused of having a screw loose. I guess I've earned that wild and crazy reputation. Sometimes my behavior borders on the bizarre. I have had so many unique, out-of-the-ordinary experiences over the years that lots of people have said, "You should write a book." Well, this is the book.

With a varied background that includes sports, business, broadcasting and ministry I have accumulated quite a collection of humorous true stories that hopefully will encourage and inspire. One thing is for sure – I've never been accused of being normal. But hey, Moses started out as a basket case and he turned out okay so there's hope for you and me.

Enjoy the book.

A man went into a restaurant and told the waitress,
"I'd like the turtle soup, and make it snappy!"

2

CHIFFOROBE

Kenny took off his ball cap and clutched it in his hands at his waist. He dug one foot at the pavement and nervously looked down. Then he said it, something so dumb, that if you had been scripting a movie you couldn't have written a more awful line, with worse timing.

I met Kenny Kessinger at a party many years ago and we instantly hit it off. You know how sometimes you have an instant rapport with someone and you have this sense that this is the start of a life-long friendship? Hasn't this happened to you with a roommate, neighbor, church member or army buddy? You become instant friends, and then although the months and miles may separate you, whenever you see each other again you easily pick up where you left off. It's like one long sentence – one long continuous comfortable conversation. I thank God for friendships. An old proverb aptly says, "With friends joy is double joy and sorrow is half a sorrow."

Kenny has good ol' country boy ways – an Elvis like boyish charm and a good-natured easygoing style. He reminds friends of Andy Griffith during the old black and white Mayberry days. Kenny, his beautiful wife Paula and their two children, Andrea and Erica, are like a television family. They all have the good looks of catalogue models and they are a down to earth all-American family.

Everyone is welcome at the Kessingers and they make everyone feel loved and special. It is no wonder that their home was the favorite hangout for Andrea and Erica's friends.

Five minutes after Kenny and I were introduced, he received a phone call. It was someone answering an ad he had in the classifieds of the local paper. Because the plant where he worked had temporarily laid off workers to retool, Kenny had decided to earn some extra money doing odd jobs. He had a brand new pickup and, ever the ambitious one, he had placed an ad that read, "Odd jobs, cleanup, have truck for hauling."

The lady on the phone asked if he could move an antique chifforobe, an old wardrobe that people used before houses had closets. After he assured her that yes he could handle the job and yes he was responsible, he agreed to move it the next day. He hung up the phone and invited me to go along for the ride.

We went to the lady's home, and it was obvious that she was wealthy. She explained that her family was moving across town and wanted the chifforobe moved separately. The woman explained in no uncertain terms that this was a family heirloom – it had belonged to her great-great-grandparents and had survived the Civil War. It was priceless and she needed assurance that Kenny was reliable, responsible and competent. "Yes ma'am," Kenny assured her in his shy polite country boy manner.

The chifforobe was massive – 7 or 8 feet tall, with beautiful beveled glass and ornate delicate wood molding. I helped Kenny load it in the back of his pick-up truck and he tied it securely with ropes. I was not a paid helper, just a new friend along for the ride. The lady once again expressed her concern for the chifforobe's safety, then said she'd meet us across town at their new house.

We started down the road. Kenny was going only 20 mph, but because the furniture loomed so large in the back of the truck, I was nervous. I cautioned him to slow down. Further down the road I again cautioned him to slow down. We were only crawling along, but the chifforobe was as aerodynamic as a skyscraper and I could hear it thumping as the wind buffeted it. I meekly suggested again to Kenny that he slow down, not wanting to offend him. I later learned that he was a seat-belt-and-road-flare kind of man, while normally I am a risk-taker – an "I-think-we-can-go-another-100-miles-on-these-tires" kind of guy. Nevertheless, I was convinced we needed to go slower.

My worst fears came true. The rope broke and the chifforobe went airborne out of the back of the truck. When it landed, glass was breaking and wood was splintering. As it hit the pavement the rope snagged it just enough to allow it to slide back and forth across the highway.

Kenny pulled over to the side of the road and collapsed on the steering wheel. "OH NO, OH NO, NO, NO, NO," he started to moan from deep down. It sounded like labor pains. I thought he was having a baby. I quickly distanced myself from my new friend. *Thank the Lord I'm not getting paid*, I thought. *I'm an innocent bystander. I'm along for the ride. I don't have a horse in this race.*

Fella I feel bad for you, but I'm thinking of my own skin. As much as I hate to admit it, I'm so glad it's you and not me! I was so glad that I was out of the loop.

We got out of the truck and quickly gathered the pieces and continued the long trip across town. We pulled into a posh neighborhood. We found the address, and there was the lady standing in the driveway anticipating our arrival.

Don't ask me why, but Kenny backed in. To give her a better look I guess. The lady spotted the chifforobe and let out a shriek. She started to approach it with outstretched hands, then backed off, then repeated the process. She was understandably horrified, and then she uttered a blood-curdling scream. She started mumbling something about the Civil War. She spun around a time or two. She had one hand in the air – in a Fred Sanford sort of way – and one hand over her mouth. At one point she was laughing and crying at the same time, and then guttural sounds came from somewhere deep in her throat. (When we were growing up, my mama threatened us kids that we would drive her to have a conniption fit. That day in the driveway of that poor woman's house, I finally saw one!)

Honestly, I did feel bad for her. Can you imagine what she was going through? I had to turn away several times, because I just couldn't bear to watch. Finally after having a miniature nervous breakdown the poor lady calmed down just a bit. In that moment – it was like being in the eye of the storm – Kenny took off his ball cap and clutched it in his hands at his waist. He dug one foot at the pavement and nervously looked down.

Then he said it, something so dumb, that if you had been scripting a movie you couldn't have written a more awful line, with worse timing. He looked up, bit his bottom lip, gestured towards the lady and said meekly, "Well ma'am, ya don't owe me nothing."

The woman went ballistic, "Don't owe you! Don't owe you!" The eye of the storm had passed and we had entered a category 5 storm. She screamed profanity so long and so loud that it would have made a sailor blush. She ordered us off her property and literally held on to Kenny's door handle and as we slowly drove away she was leaning in the cab cussing him for all he was worth.

That was my initial introduction to Mr. Kenny

Kessinger. I knew right then and there that this ol' boy needed help. I decided right on the spot to be his life long friend, to keep him out of trouble (or was it the other way around). That temporary moving assignment over 20 years ago was our first adventure together. But believe me, it wasn't to be our last.

———◆•◆◆———

Make sure that the priceless things in your life are tightly secured. Tie up loose ends and make sure that all the knots in your life are tight. The Marines' term for this is to be "squared away." Life is too precious and too fragile to take unnecessary risks.

Let us hear the conclusion of the whole matter: Fear God, and keep his commandments: for this *is* the whole duty of man (Ecclesiastes 12: 13 KJV).

If at first you don't succeed…so much for skydiving.

3

THE DUMP TRUCK

Adam was nearly 20 feet up in the air. He was hanging from the edge, dangling and screaming, "Help! Uncle J. J. , help! Please help!"

I moved from Kentucky to Mississippi in 1985. Shortly after the move, my sister Kelly came for a visit and brought my three nephews along. A friend of mine brought her two children over to greet my sister.

When she arrived after the three hundred mile road trip, Kelly had no sooner pulled in the driveway when she and my friend greeted each other and immediately decided they would go to the mall. They turned to me and declared, "We're going shopping and you're going to baby-sit." When my face registered my surprise, Kelly added, "We'll just be gone an hour – it won't kill you!" This all happened quicker than you can say – Play Doh.

I'd never really been around children much. It was scary and a little intimidating to be surrounded by five children – several of whom were very young. We're talking about little ankle-biters, crumb-eaters and curtain-climbers. I felt as out of place as a TV dinner at a church potluck.

Now, you have to consider my dilemma. I had never been married and had no children. Close family and friends had long since given up on the notion and thought if matrimony ever did catch up with me, instead of putting a "Just married" sign on the back of the get-away car, someone should place one that said, "Finally married."

Since there was an absence of the pitter-patter of little feet around my house, I had no children's toys. I mean I didn't have a *single* toy – no sandbox, no swing set, nothing! I was drawing a blank on how to spend those 60 long minutes.

I spotted the solution in the backyard – my dump truck! I had a part-time tree trimming business, and owned a one-ton dump truck with a steel gravel bed. To me that dump truck started looking like six flags over Mississippi! I thought, *I'll just put them in the back of the truck, raise the bed, dump 'em out onto the grass and it'll be like a giant sliding board.*

There didn't seem to be any way for them to get hurt, because the sides and floor were slick sheet metal, and with the tail gate down the kids would just slide right out. Sure, it sounds bizarre, but it made perfect sense to Mr. Bachelor Boy.

"Do you want me to dump you out of the dump truck?" I asked. They looked over at the truck and scratched their little heads. They seemed a bit apprehensive, but when they all said "Yes." I smiled and said, "Well, get in!"

I piled them in the back and as I started raising the bed, no one came out! Up and up it went, and still no one! I guess they had found rivets and seams to cling to. It's amazing how strong little kids fingernails are. A few had sort of super glued their little selves into the corner, wedged in tight.

The bed went even higher and finally – the law of gravity took over – out they came. I could hear them tumbling and see them sliding down. They were dropping like flies from the sides. The holdouts had a pretty rough ride due to the initial two-foot drop into the bed, but hey, it's the price you pay for being stubborn. If they had stayed limber, relaxed, and enjoyed the ride, they could have slid and tumbled out effortlessly. (This rings a bell. Didn't they teach us in Drivers Ed to relax and stay limber when you realize an automobile accident is inevitable?) Who knows? It may even help 'em out someday if they have rodeo ambitions – eight seconds of holding on for dear life is really not all that long.

They had all tumbled out except Adam, who at eight or nine was the oldest. With the bed raised all the way up, Adam was nearly 20 feet up in the air. He was hanging from the edge, dangling and screaming, "Help! Uncle J. J., help! Please help!" I couldn't believe he was able to still hold on – and to this day, I'm not sure what he was holding on to.

I rolled the truck forward a bit and stomped on the brake. The bed shook, jarring him loose, and he slid on out. (Well, I did roll *forward*. It's not like I was going to back the dump truck up! C'mon, I'm smarter than I look.)

I ran around to the back of the truck to check on the astronauts. They were wadded together, clinging to each other for all they were worth. They sort of looked like shipwreck victims, quivering, sniffling, huddled together wide eyed and mildly traumatized.

I said, "Nobody got hurt, relax. You're all okay, everything's all right, no damage done."

They continued to whimper, but when I asked them, "You wanna go again?" Immediately the sniffling stopped and they shrieked a collective, "YEAH!"

I loaded them in and dumped them out, loaded them in and dumped them out, over and over. I did this the whole time the mamas were shopping. Curious on-lookers started to slow their cars down in front of my house, and neighbors were peeking through their mini-blinds, watching me operate this redneck amusement ride in my driveway in broad daylight.

This story is *sad* but true. Now I suppose some of you are nearly horrified right about now, and perhaps you're thinking, *What kind of half-wit would baby-sit small children using a dump truck?* Well, you sort of answered your own question. You're right, it takes someone without a lick of sense to pull a half-baked stunt like that. And now that I have children of my own, I shudder when I realize how irresponsible my actions were – and will probably never do it again.

Finally, the moms arrived. Boy, they were *not* impressed with my babysitting techniques! They questioned my upbringing and my sanity. I won't repeat all the unkind names they called me, but I will say this…they never asked me to baby-sit again!

Do you think the people on "cloud 8" can hear the people on "cloud 9" having a good time?

4
FIRST FLIGHT

I can never remember not wanting to fly. Maybe psychiatrists are right, and those episodes of the television show, "Sky King," I viewed as a preschooler sowed aviation seeds early on. As far back as I can remember I've passionately wanted to fly an airplane.

A few times during high school, my dates actually consisted of a drive to the airport to watch the airplanes. We would grab some burgers, and park by the fence beside the runway in hopes that an airplane – any airplane – would take off or land. Looking back, I'm sure the poor girls were probably bored to tears, but I can still remember the excitement I felt when one of those big birds came in for a landing, lights blinking, engine whining, strobe lights flashing. Wow! It all seemed bigger than life.

Later, working on construction sites, whenever a plane would fly over I'd declare to my co-workers, "You see that airplane? I'll be up there one day. I'm gonna learn how to fly! That'll be me up there and I'll be the one doing the driving."

I must have mentioned it a lot because eventually when I would start with, "One of these days...," my co-workers would say, "Yeah, yeah, we know, you're gonna fly a plane."

Actually, one time my friend Glen Edwards and I signed

up for ground school and attended a couple of classes, but we quickly realized it would be too expensive. After moving to Tupelo, Mississippi, however, I decided it was time. I was going to get my pilot's license!

I paid a visit to the Fixed Base Operation (FBO) of our local airport. An FBO is like a full service gas station for airplanes. Along with fuel, they provide aircraft rental and flight instruction. I'll bet you didn't realize that you can actually rent an airplane. *Rental plane.* Now there's a comforting thought. Think for a moment how rental cars are treated. Now, multiply that by 5,000 feet.

After introducing myself to the clerk at the front desk, I inquired about learning to fly. They explained the requirements to obtain a pilot's certificate. Basically, in addition to ground school, you need only forty hours of actual flight time to earn a pilot's license.

Now there's another comforting thought. It takes 1,600 hours to become a cosmetologist, 1,600 hours to learn to cut hair, and only 40 hours to operate an airplane! I mean, what's the worst mistake your stylist can make? Do you know the difference between a bad haircut and a good one? About two weeks. Hey, your hair will grow back, but a pilot in command of an aircraft zooming across the sky over your city after only 40 hours! Wow, now that's scary.

At the FBO, after we discussed the requirements, they introduced me to an instructor and invited me to come back when I was ready to begin. After a couple of weeks passed, I had scraped some money together and showed up one Saturday morning for my very first flying lesson. Actually, this would be my first flight in a small airplane. I had only flown a couple of times *as a passenger* in a commercial jet. The instructor I had met weeks earlier was not there but the person at the counter pointed out several instructors huddled around the coffee pot in the back and asked if they would suffice.

I said, "Sure."

The clerk shouted out, "Hey any of you guys have time to go up with a student?" One instructor approached, then we shook hands and walked outside to the tarmac.

You know, after a lifetime of attending seminars I've noticed two recurring themes for successful living. One is that we should always strive to remember people's names. (I learned this at a *Dave* Carnegie seminar.) The other is the importance of communication. Communication is stressed in every seminar of any kind. Yes, communication is key. Well, a terrible breakdown in communication occurred right then and there, but I was completely oblivious at the time.

The instructor assumed I was a student with 20 or 30 hours, but I had literally never seen a small airplane up close! I should have been alarmed when after a pre-flight walk-around inspection of the plane, he told me to get in on the driver's side! Then he requested that I start the pre-flight procedures in the cockpit. I must have had that proverbial "deer in the headlights" look on my face because he graciously offered to do it for me to save some time all the while mumbling something about me being nervous.

"Okay, start it up," he ordered.

Start it up?!? I thought, *Fella, this is an AIRPLANE!* But I said nothing, and many other thoughts immediately began jockeying for the pole position on the racetrack of my mind. *Wow, they are serious about you getting your money's worth for these lessons. I guess if you're going to get a license in only 40 hours, it has to be an accelerated program. But it sure is happening quickly. It doesn't quite seem right. Then again, who am I to argue? He's the teacher, I'm the pupil.*

He's the boss, I'm the peon. He's the veteran, I'm the rookie. So surely he knows what he's doing. This is all foreign to me. I'm just doing what I'm told.

Those few moments seemed like a short lifetime. Ever notice how relevant time is – "a couple of minutes" means different things to different people – it depends on which side of the bathroom door you're on.

"Well," he said, "Start it up and there's the key in the ignition."

I'm just obeying orders, so, *here goes nothing.* Something in my gut kept telling me that something's bad wrong here, but this ol' Kentucky boy is just dumb enough to twist the key and start the airplane. It roared to life and with the propeller spinning wildly, started lunging forward.

"Brakes! Brakes!" the instructor screamed over the engine noise.

I looked down at the floorboard and there were two pedals, so I just started stomping. Again, a myriad of thoughts flooded my mind. *Shouldn't we have watched a film, looked at some charts or had some kind of orientation? This is just plain crazy!*

My thoughts were interrupted by the instructor's command to taxi to the runway. *Taxi? What is taxi?* My mind continued to race. *Taxi to the runway and do what? Ease out on the runway and pop the clutch? This just doesn't feel right. Maybe, I should say something.*

At the edge of the runway the instructor asked me to do a "run-up." Of course, as a pilot I now know what that expression means, but at that moment I didn't have a clue. I must have had that calf staring at a new gate expression, because he once again said something about me probably being nervous and he'd just do it to save me some time.

With the run-up complete, he said, "Okay, push the throttle forward."

My heart was hammering at this point, my nostrils flared and my eyes were wide open. The veins on my neck must have been bulging like Barney Fife's. The Lamaze instructors would have been proud of how I was breathing. I was wide-awake, with all senses razor sharp. I wondered, *if aviation training is this concentrated, what is Green Beret training like or how do they treat physicians on their first day of med school? Does someone in a lab coat greet them with a clipboard in hand, declaring, "Oh, so this is your first day. Alright, go down to room 107 and get started on that appendectomy. Just get as far as you can and I'll be down shortly to check on your progress!"*

The instructor broke my train of thought by shouting, "Firewall it, let's get this puppy up in the air!"

I floored it, and we sling-shotted down the runway, engine howling and wind whistling. I love adventure, but I knew I was in way over my head. Palms sweaty, heart racing, I wondered if I was going to pass out or have a heart attack or something. I had concerns about my laundry bill going up! When we started racing down the runway it looked pretty wide, but towards the end with the increased speed it seemed like we were on a narrow sidewalk.

"Okay, pull back on the yoke," he said.

I assumed that must be the steering wheel. I yanked the steering wheel – uh, the yoke – all the way back. The plane shot up like a rocket.

The instructor began frantically screaming, "Lower the nose! Lower the nose!"

I pushed it all the way forward causing the airplane to suddenly dive.

"Raise the nose! Raise the nose!"he yelled again.

I pulled her all the way back and we went nearly straight up again.

This wild roller coaster action continued until we finally leveled off. There were several moments of silence. He then pointed and said, "Turn to a heading of 090 degrees." I just looked which way his finger was pointing and steered accordingly. We were flying along, I had a death-grip on the yoke. I don't remember what I was thinking or feeling at this point. After you hold your breath for so long you get a little lightheaded and it affects your short-term memory.

He then asked if I minded if he smoked. I consented. So he lit up a cigarette, looked out the window, and appeared not to have a care in the world. Now, here is when it got comical. He casually asked, "So how long have you been flying?"

With my voice an octave too high and cracking I sounded like a teenager going through an adolescent growth spurt, I managed to squeak, "This is my first lesson."

From the corner of my eye, I saw him spit out his cigarette and then barely catch it between his fingers. He said some words I won't print here, and shouted, "What? Get outta here! You've gotta be kidding." He was visibly shaken.

I replied, "I wish I was 'cause you've just about scared me to death." I was so nearly traumatized I was blinking back tears.

Because of the break-neck speed in which this had all unfolded I would not have been surprised if at some point he had reached behind the seat to retrieve a parachute and announced, "Well I've got a two o'clock appointment. I'm going to go on out the door and you can make it back to the airport the best way you can." There was more silence – he must have been thinking about what *could* have happened, if we had stalled, etc. Finally he broke the silence and said, "Well, you're not doing half bad. You wanna keep on flying the airplane?" Still unable to muster a single baritone note I squeaked, "Sure." We flew a little longer and then thankfully he landed the plane.

That would have been a good day to start taking nitro-glycerin tablets, but I didn't. I actually continued flying and finally, after many starts and stops, over several years, I earned my private pilot's license in November 1995. I'm glad I did because of the joys, rewards and freedom of flying. There is a feeling that is hard to describe when you strap yourself into a cockpit, sizzle down a runway and then lift off. You are the one behind the controls, you are flying! There is an incredible sense of freedom, your cares seem to slip behind you as suddenly as the runway disappears beneath your wing. I've flown the length of the Ozark Mountains, flown at night over the Gulf of Mexico watching the coastal lights flicker and dance. I've seen spectacular sunrises and sunsets. I've flown alone on a clear starry night, listening to the drone of the engine, with an unobstructed view, reminded of what the Psalmist said, "The heavens declare the glory of God; the skies proclaim the work of His hands."

Flying is a unique opportunity to have a bird's eye view of God's incredible creation. Of all the thrills and adventures I've experienced, piloting an aircraft is second to none. I can never remember not wanting to fly.

There is a time to be assertive. There is no such thing as a dumb question, if your family, your health or your safety is at risk. Have the courage to say no when necessary. Never let anyone intimidate you into doing something you know isn't right.

Suspenders are the oldest form of social security.

5
RADIO AND MUSIC

My two sisters, Kelly and Karen, are the only ones on this planet that knew of my secret desire to be a D. J. They caught me red-handed "doing radio" using a comb for a microphone. You singers reading this may have gotten busted a time or two singing to a shampoo bottle or doing some comb-singing yourself.

It's interesting, because I didn't actually pursue a radio career, but according to Psalm 37: 4, "God gives us the desires of our heart." I began my broadcasting career in 1985 with WCFB radio in Tupelo, Mississippi. I have been the on-air morning personality with American Family Radio since I joined in 1991, and American Family Radio is the fastest-growing network of any radio format in broadcasting history.

While being a morning on-air personality is my day job, on weekends I do stand-up comedy and public speaking events. Add to that schedule, my responsibilities as a husband and father and I sometimes feel like that guy who keeps the plates spinning on their sticks all the while whistling Dixie through a harmonica on a neck brace. I think you can see I have a full schedule, but I'm not complaining. It still amazes me how God took many of the loves of my life – radio, music, humor and people – and wove them together into a fulfilling career.

Often when I meet people, they share that they, too, think that they would enjoy being "on-air." Maybe you've even thought about it. But I want you to think this thing through, because it requires a very unusual personality type to be a D. J.

Just consider the working conditions. You sit in a room and yak-and-yak – to no one you can see. You tell jokes *and* laugh out loud – but no one is in the room with you. Oh, you might reason, it's just like talking on the phone with a friend. But not really. At least someone on the phone says, "Yeah, uh huh," occasionally.

Just think what might happen if you did these "on-air" things in a different setting. Say, on a park bench while feeding pigeons. And there you are, telling jokes and laughing and talking to someone you can't see – they would throw a net over you and haul you to the home for the permanently bewildered.

Oh, and there's one more clue about on-air personalities – the room where we work…it's padded! (Sure it's padded for acoustics, but it *is* a padded room.)

There is something else you should understand about being a disc jockey – it's tougher than it may sound. In broadcasting school, they teach that if you have what it takes to be a D. J. , you have to be able to say "toy boat" ten times, out loud, real fast. We have the time if you'd like to take the test. All you need to do to see if you're made of the right stuff is to quickly say, "toy boat," out loud, ten times in a row. Are you ready? Okay, let's take the test. Remember – *out loud* and *quickly* say, "Toy boat," ten times. I'll wait. Ready, set, go.

How did you do? That's called job security, my friend.

Like I said – it's tougher to be a D. J. than you may suppose. Oh, and by the way, I made up the part about that being taught in broadcasting school. How would I know – I've never been!

But I do enjoy being a broadcaster. For almost 20 years, I've had the privilege through radio to hopefully influence, encourage and inspire listeners. It's rewarding to be an early morning cheerleader for Jesus. Add to that doing live remotes, interviews, traveling, and the many radio friendships I've made over the years, and basically I've had a job where I get paid to listen to music, drink coffee and love people. I would do it for free – and unfortunately, my boss knows that.

Like many Americans, I grew up listening to the radio. I agree with Wayne Pederson, Chairman of National Religious Broadcasters, who said that radio is a wonderful part of our culture. Back before my day, families sat in the living room and "watched" the radio.

In the 1950's television replaced radio as the source of drama and comedy. However, radio survived and began the new era of music and disc jockeys. The transistor radio enhanced the "take-along ability" of radios, enabling people to "be there" with music, news, weather and sports.

Radio is known as "the theater of the mind." Without the distraction of scenery, sets and lights, the radio offers a blank page for listeners to use their imagination and relate and participate in a uniquely personal way.

When Charles Osgood signed off with "see you on the radio," he attested to the power of radio to imagine things only the mind can see. Years ago a popular radio ad described in great detail a colorful story, and then ended by saying, "Can you imagine that? You just did – you saw it on the radio."

That's what makes radio so powerful. Orson Welles turned the novel *War of the Worlds* into a radio broadcast and sent Americans into a panic. Stan Freeberg dropped his 2,000-pound marshmallow into Lake Michigan, which had been drained and filled with hot chocolate.

Radio is the most intimate medium. Listeners invite you into the privacy of their homes while they are getting ready for work and school. They travel in their vehicles while listening to the radio – often alone with the D. J. Sometimes, when people are having a sleepless night, they'll get out of bed and turn on their constant, trusted companion, the radio.

Not only is radio the most intimate of mediums, it is the only one that doesn't require a line of sight. You have to watch the TV, read newspapers, look at the computer, etc. But radio provides a wonderful backdrop to daily life. You can enjoy background music while you do most anything.

While radio is news, entertainment, sports and weather, when most people think of radio, they probably think of music. And boy, do I love music. I was invited to teach a university workshop on the effects of music in our lives. Before the bell rings, I hope we have time for a short lecture. Now class, sit up straight and pay attention – there may be a quiz.

I believe we underestimate the effects of music in our lives. Music helps set moods. It enhances movies – listen to the background music in a mystery movie or action thriller. Music can evoke certain memories. You can hear a song and remember where you were and what you were doing during that summer of long ago when you first heard that favorite tune. Music is so moving and so powerful, it can make us laugh or cry. Have you ever found yourself absent-mindedly humming a tune that you didn't intentionally memorize and you can't seem to get out of your head?

Music communicates more powerfully than mere words. Almost no one realizes the power of music in their life. The ancient Greeks were so moved by it that they ascribed it to gods called "muses," from which our word "music" comes. Plato spent only two pages of his *Republic* on the economics of the ideal state, but forty pages on its music! He said that if that ideal state ever came into existence, it would decay when its music began to decay. (I personally have never read any of Plato's works – it doesn't have enough pictures for me. Uh, oh, I just realized this book doesn't have any pictures, either.) One historian wrote that every major political revolution of modern times was preceded by a musical revolution.

I'm convinced that music teaches, music sells and music affects us deeply. We grew up learning numbers and our ABC's with sing-along tunes. Madison Avenue advertisers know that a catchy tune will catapult their sales pitch in an ad. During times like the Super Bowl they bet in excess of a million dollars that if they can have just 30 seconds of your time, throw in a couple of fun sound bites and combine that with a catchy tune, they will influence you. You may not jump up and run out and buy their product immediately, but they gamble (and win) millions of dollars hoping that music will eventually help sell a product. Yes, music teaches, music sells and music affects us. I'm convinced we absolutely underestimate the effects and influence of music in our lives.

I love radio and I love music. I'm thankful I have a career in Christian radio. Secular music isn't all bad, but although it may not be blatantly evil, it helps reinforce philosophies and values and perspectives that often leave God out. We must carefully guard what we watch and hear. A friend of mine was criticized because he limits the amount of prime-time TV and secular music he allows his children to digest. When challenged as to why he wouldn't allow it, he said, "For the same reason I won't let my children drink out of the toilet!" Good point.

On the other hand Christian music glorifies Jesus Christ and embraces Christian values. In God's word it says, "Speak to one another with psalms, hymns and spiritual songs. Sing and make music in your heart to the Lord," (Ephesians 5: 19). It also says, "Let the word of Christ dwell in you richly as you teach and admonish one another with all wisdom, and as you sing psalms, hymns and spiritual songs with gratitude in your hearts to God,"(Colossians 3:16).

These biblical passages reveal how important Christian music should be in the lives of every Christian. In fact, the longest book in the Bible – Psalms – is a *songbook*.

We know that godly music was vital to the life of the Old Testament believer. After God delivered the Israelites from the Egyptians, the first thing they did after crossing the Red Sea was to sing a song of praise to the Lord. They ultimately gave thanks, prayed and built an altar, but the first thing they did was to sing (Exodus 15).

The Old Testament also shows us that God's music is a great influence during our spiritual conflicts. Throughout the Old Testament, music is associated with victory. Songs of praise accompanied the triumphs of godly people like Deborah (Judges 5), Moses (Numbers 21: 16-18), David (1 Chronicles 15: 16-28), Nehemiah (Nehemiah 12: 27-31, 38-43), and others. And on occasion, as the tribes of Israel were going up against their enemies, God's instructions were to put the choir and musical instruments in *front* of the army.

As we've already seen, the New Testament stresses music, too. As James says, "Is anyone cheerful: Let him sing praises," (James 5: 13).

Through the ages, music has proven to be an excellent tool to help people set their minds and hearts on God. The benefits of Christian music in the believer's life are many.

Since the music on Christian radio comes in a variety of styles and sounds, why not listen to a positive alternative?

I am grateful to Dr. Donald E. Wildmon for giving me an opportunity in national radio, and I am also thankful to you, the listener. I am humbled when I read the encouraging mail I receive from people all across America who tell me they listen to me on American Family Radio around the breakfast table, in their vehicles, and at work. You make me feel more like a family member than a radio friend. I really love my listeners and I hope that comes across on-air.

If you do not listen to American Family Radio, I invite you to listen at www. afr. net or please call and ask for a station listing guide.

Obviously, I *believe* in Christian radio – it's music and programming that is wholesome, positive and Christ-centered. It's music with a message. God bless you, and I'll see you on the radio.

---

* Research for notes on music were gleaned from a wide variety of published stories, articles and bible studies collected over a fifteen-year period, including excerpts from works by Al Menconi, Bob Larson and others.

The early bird gets the worm, but it's the second
mouse that gets the cheese.

6

PRACTICAL JOKES

Ron Shank is absolutely the funniest person I've ever met in my entire life. Those of you who know him are nodding your head in agreement. That guy is an absolute nut!

We once worked together at American Family Radio. I remember one time he made a label and placed it on the soap dispenser in the men's room. The computer-generated label looked authentic. It appeared factory made and there on the soap dispenser it read, "Do not rinse with water."

Ed Vitagliano, another co-worker, happened in shortly after the label appeared. After instinctively getting one or two squirts of soap from the dispenser he spied the label. "What the…? Oh man, this is just great," he fumed, "What in the world – If not with water then with what?"

I was the fly on the stall wall and witnessed the entire incident. And it just so happened that we were out of paper towels. (Thank you, Mr. Murphy, for your wonderful law.) Turning from side to side with soapy hands raised you could see and hear his frustration. I don't remember if he wiped the suds on his pant legs or not, because I was too busy laughing at all of the commotion.

I'm not too keen on practical jokes, I'm really not. I enjoy a funny story or a good clean joke but I'm not too big on practical jokes because they can too easily backfire. Plus as a general rule, I don't enjoy getting a laugh at someone else's expense. However, there was that one time when someone had given me a *very real* looking, rubber snake. It was so lifelike, dark on top and lighter on the bottom. That dude was made of some kind of high tech industrial strength rubber, because when you threw it on the ground it quivered and wriggled for several seconds after you dropped it. Man, it looked real!

I noticed my good-natured, next-door neighbor, Mitchell Brazeal, faithfully working every evening building a garage behind his house. Low lying tree limbs allowed him limited room to work. Late one evening I broke my no-practical-joke rule and decided to drape the snake on the limbs exactly where Mitch would start working the next day. I actually thought the joke might not work. The wind might cause the snake to fall or maybe Mitch wouldn't even notice, but it was worth a try to have a little harmless fun.

I had forgotten about the snake until several days later. I was getting ready for bed and after my nightly routine, I pulled back the covers and got snuggled in just right. I rolled over to one side just a bit when my leg bumped something cold and clammy. I screamed like a junior high girl. Then all in one motion threw back the covers, snatched up whatever frog, mouse or creature was about to devour me and leaped from the bed. I felt like one of those cartoon characters whose feet spin around several times in the air before they actually make ground contact.

It was the rubber snake! I never used to lock my doors, so the payback required little effort on Mitch's part. Since Mitch scared me out of my wits, then I assumed that he'd obviously found it. Had my plan worked?

I asked him how he discovered the snake, hoping it

startled him at least a little. A *little*? You couldn't have scripted it better in a movie. He was working in the strategic spot under the tree limbs. Friends had come over to grill out. With their friends by her side, his wife Nancy called for him to please finish and come start the grill! With an audience in the yard looking on, Mitch took a step back and bumped the limbs. The snake fell from the tree and draped around his neck. Mitch ran (screaming like a junior high girl, I hope!) toward his friends, frantically trying to pull the snake off. He swears to this day the snake bit him three times. He finally unwrapped the tangled snake from around his neck and threw it on the ground, grabbed a hoe and proceeded to "kill" the rubber snake. He probably owes me a month's gym membership – think of the great cardiovascular workout he received!

I actually got more mileage from the snake by trying to settle a score with Steve Chapman. Steve and Annie are talented singer-songwriters, who Dr. James Dobson refers to as musical ambassadors to the family. Steve, Annie and their children, Nathan and Heidi, are the epitome of a Christian family – I've never met a finer family than theirs.

As a stand-up Christian comedian, I have been privileged to open for them in concert on many occasions. Once, in the lobby of a hotel after breakfast while on the road, Steve asked me how I liked the hotel service and if I had gotten a good night's sleep.

"No," I said, "Somebody kept waking me up all night, calling my room. I got several different calls – at 3 a.m., 4 a.m. and 5 a.m."

Steve inquired if it had ever happened before. I said, "As a matter of fact, yes. I don't know what their problem is, but it seems like once or twice a year the same thing happens in different cities."

I never noticed the twinkle in Steve's eye. Steve – who has an incredible sense of humor – said, "You just don't get it, do you? I've been doing this to you for years. When we are on the road together, I call the front desk, tell them I'm you and ask for multiple early morning wake up calls."

Well, Steve was right. Sometimes I don't get it. You ever have those days where you feel like you're not the sharpest knife in the drawer? One fry short of a happy meal? The wheel's turnin' but the hamster's dead? Steve had been pulling these pranks for years and I had no clue. Well the mystery was solved and we both had a good laugh.

Sometime later, Steve and his daughter, Heidi, were embarking on a bike ride. They were riding from Tupelo, Mississippi, to Nashville, Tennessee, so I convinced them to spend the night at my house. Late that night after they had gone to bed, I remembered Steve's wake up calls and remembered the snake! I rummaged through a number of boxes, found the snake and stuffed him in Steve's bedrolls under his saddlebags.

The next day, after a long day's bike ride, it was beginning to get dark, rainy and foggy. Before the bottom fell out of the weather, Steve quickly scrambled to make camp with darkness falling. It couldn't have worked out better: as he opened the bedroll, the snake fell out and landed right on his feet. Thankfully, the many years of Steve's gun safety habits prevented him from shooting a good toe off.

Much later, at the 20-year American Family Association anniversary celebration banquet, I stood to speak, flanked by Larry Burkett and Dr. Donald E. Wildmon, along with the Chapmans and others at the head table. After my short speech and a roast for Dr. Wildmon, I returned to my seat. I started to sit down and saw *the* snake, coiled in my chair. It's a small wonder I didn't leap off the stage into the audience. That night was the last I saw of the snake. (You don't still have it do you Steve? Are you plotting something?)We got a lot of mileage outta that little rubber fella.

One spring my wife and I decided to travel with her family to California. Eight of us drove in a seven-passenger van from the Mississippi Gulf Coast to southern California. The trip would have been as bad as it sounds, except I love my in-laws – they're terrific. They are one of the most fun, creative, well-balanced, godly families you'll ever meet.

Because my father-in-law, Lowry Anderson, is the rugged, macho type, I assumed he would drive the first leg of the trip and, like most men, not be quick to relinquish his post behind the wheel. I made a huge poster to tape to the back of the van. In large bold letters the poster said, "Please honk, point and wave wildly at the driver…Thanks!" (Lowry was the only one who didn't know what was going on.)

Just as I had hoped, Lowry was driving first. I made an excuse to get out of the van one last time, retrieved my poster from its hiding place beside the garage and slapped it on the back. I already had the tape on it. We merrily started on our excellent adventure.

A few blocks from the house the honkers and wavers came through. "Hey, how ya doing!" Lowry would say, then wonder out loud, "Who was that?"

For the next several blocks enthusiastic honkers and wavers kept it up. "Boy, folks sure are friendly in our town," Lowry said.

On down the road this continued, with an occasional vehicle passing with the driver honking, giving a hearty thumbs up. And Lowry kept trying to figure it out, "Is it someone from work, school? Oh, it must be someone from our Sunday school class." The class Lowry teaches has over 80 people. "I guess it could've been that visitor. That's got to be who it was," he concluded.

Well, we were all having our own private amusement party over Lowry's guess-a-thon. After we were in the next county, so many people had complied with joyous waves and smiles that Lowry began thinking that, since they had borrowed the van from Bill, one of their good friends, people must think it's Bill and his family in the vehicle. "Wow, Bill knows everybody!" Lowry said.

You can only imagine how diverse this highway "studio audience" was. Car loads of college students climbing over each other to shout and cheer. A van load of smiling nuns, truckers galore. I'm glad it brightened the day for someone to read my simple instructions, participate, and then watch a confused Lowry scratching his head, trying to decide why he was the popular traveler. A couple of times he was even fearful that the "turtle" containing our luggage on top of the van was coming loose.

Somewhere out west – I think it was in Texas, because you can drive three whole days and still be in the Lone Star state – after the umpteenth cheerleader passed, Lowry dryly said, "Okay, what's written on the back of the van?" We had a good laugh. Like I said, they're a fun family.

Another time I was flying over to meet my cousin, Kevin, and his wife, Teresa, in Tennessee. I was bringing gifts along with lots of luggage, so I instructed Kevin to find out the keypad combination to open the gate at the airport and drive out and meet me on the tarmac, where it would be easy to unload the airplane right next to the car.

I was touching down at the tiny unmanned airport in Linden, southwest of Nashville in Tennessee hill country, and I spotted Kevin, right on time there beside the taxiway. After exchanging hugs and hellos we unloaded the plane and started to drive out. As we approached the gate Kevin noticed there was no keypad inside and, slightly alarmed, said, "Oh, no, the gate is closed and the keypad is out front. What're we gonna do? How will we climb over the fence – it's topped with barbed wire?"

What he didn't realize is that there *is* no keypad inside, because it's automatic. You just drive right up to the fence and stop approximately two feet from the gate. There must be a sensor under the pavement or perhaps a laser beam that triggers it, but it's automatic.

I'll have some fun, I thought as we approached the gate. "Just push in your cigarette lighter," I said.

"Push in the lighter? Why?" he asked.

I replied, "Just push it in and watch."

He pushed it in as we rolled to a stop in front of the gate. I was hoping that the timing would at least be close, but in fact it was perfect. We stopped and as if on cue – the exact second the lighter popped out – the gate made its clankety, clank, clank sounds and opened automatically.

"What in the? How do they…what in the world?" Kevin was saying, unable to finish his sentences. He was pointing at the lighter, then pointing to the gate then back to the lighter.

"Just drive, Kevin," I said.

With the gate closing behind us, Kevin was still puzzled, shaking his head. He asked, "But a cigarette lighter! What signal sets it off? I mean, how…why?"

I interrupted, "Man, I don't understand all that. I still can't program a VCR, but you know how they are with all this high tech stuff. Hey, if they can put a man on the moon then this is easy, light weight, electronics-wise."

I was enjoying the fun, and Kevin had an expression like a puppy when you blow in his face. But still Kevin wouldn't quit trying to figure it out, he stammered, "Well, I mean… I wonder… I mean, how… Well, what's a guy gonna do if he doesn't have a cigarette lighter?"

Out of nowhere the bogus answer comes to me. "Hey, I guess they figure, if a guy's got enough money to fly airplanes then he's gonna be able to afford a vehicle that has a cigarette lighter in it."

Kevin's shoulders shrugged his approval, and the nod of his head along with the raised eyebrows, concluded that he finally agreed with the answer. He was satisfied then. We drove to his place and had a great weekend visit.

When I was leaving, with the plane loaded and after saying our goodbyes, I started going over the airplane checklist and Kevin got in his car to leave. Then it dawned on me I had never told him any different about the airport gate! Boy, just in the nick of time, I caught him before he left. If I hadn't told him and he had stopped too far from whatever really triggers the fence, he could have still been there playing with the cigarette lighter while you're reading this book. I told him the truth and we both laughed long and loud. It doesn't happen often, but those deep down robust belly laughs are good for you.

I've just realized how I started this chapter. In the beginning, I explained how I'm not keen on practical jokes, and honestly I'm not. Well, if I don't necessarily believe in practical jokes, then why would I devote an *entire* chapter to them? I don't know what to say or do now. I've painted myself in a corner. Have you ever started telling a co-worker a funny joke and close to the end forgotten the punch line? That's how I'm feeling right now. Maybe there *is* a lesson here. If I don't believe in practical jokes and I wrote an entire chapter on the subject, some might argue that it makes me a hypocrite. I think it would be a stretch to conclude that, but I will confess that there are times in my life when I am hypocritical. And this much I know – being a hypocrite is no laughing matter.

As a born again believer in Jesus Christ, the one word that perhaps stings more than any other is the word hypocrite. Webster's defines a hypocrite as one who plays a part; a false pretender to virtue or piety.

Sometimes values and principals I believe with my whole heart, I don't practice. For instance, I rarely pray and read the Bible as often as I know I should. You can add to that list, fasting, sharing my faith, etc. Sometimes I fail to do things I know I should and things I detest I sometimes find myself doing, such as losing my temper, having wrong thoughts, etc. I suspect we all have areas where we struggle for consistency.

I don't want to be a hypocrite – not just for me, but I don't want to bring dishonor to the Holy One who shed His blood for me, the one in whom there is no fault or guile. Lord, help me to practice the things I preach. Help me not only to talk the talk, but to walk the walk. Because it's true, people are watching our lives and sometimes we are the only Bible they will ever read.

---•+•+•---

Corduroy pillows are making headlines

---•+•+•---

7
COTTON-PICKIN'
CHICKEN CHUNKER

Orville, Wilber and I could have been big buddies because I love to fly airplanes. Consequently, I enjoy aviation magazines. One day I was reading the March 1996 edition of the AOPA Pilot magazine and I came across this article, *Learjet in Chicken Fight.*

The article stated: "Learjet and an independent manufacturer of Learjet cockpit windshields are having a shootout, so to speak.

When Perkins Aircraft of Fort Worth, Texas, offered the windshields at $10,000 less than the Learjet parts price last year, Learjet fired back with a service information letter warning customers that the windshields were not chicken tested. That is, the FAA did not require Perkins to prove that the windshields could survive a bird impact at approximately 300 knots. To simulate the bird strike, Learjet tests its windows using a cannon that fires a chicken at 300 knots towards a stationary cockpit."

Basically, Learjet was saying that yeah, Perkins may sell cheaper windshields, but they're not "chicken tested."

In fact, there *is* a government-sanctioned chicken launcher that fires chickens at a speed of 300 knots (345 mph) at aircraft windshields to simulate a bird strike in flight. Apparently, if the airplane windshield doesn't break, fold, bend, mutilate or spindle, everything is okay. If the glass cracks, it's back to the drawing board. (I wonder what they went back to before there was a "drawing board?")

Well the article wasn't meant to amuse, but my Far Side sense of humor hijacked me. Chicken tested! Chicken cannon! I remember thinking, *Boy, just about the time you think you know what everybody does for a living…some fella in Wichita is tamping chickens down a barrel, covering his ears and blasting away at cockpit windshields eight hours a day.* How terrible, poor chickens.

As I tried to picture this operation, my imagination immediately went into overdrive and a million questions ran through my mind. Just who is running that cotton-pickin' chicken chunker anyway, Darrell or his other brother Darrell? Where did he learn to do this? What's the response when school children ask, "What does your daddy do?" Do they offer this course at the community college? Who is he pulling for? I know who's paying his salary, but it sure must get boring bouncing poultry off windshields day in and day out. Do you suppose deep down he secretly wants to occasionally see some glass shatter? What kind of ammo are they using? High velocity chickens? Low velocity? Armor piercing chickens? Scud chickens? All of these crazy notions were going through my head. What do they do with the scraps – you know, the chicken shrapnel? I'll tell you my guess. They're taking that stuff home and having fried chicken, broiled chicken, chicken potpies, chicken ala king, chicken fricassee and every other type of chicken imaginable – and some we'd never imagine.

I shared my musings with Tim Wildmon and he put them in his book, *My Life as a Half-Baked Christian.* I actually shared my thoughts "On-Air" and had an engineer from Learjet immediately contact me. Oh, no, I'm in trouble again. AGAIN is the operative word here. No one likes to have his or her mistakes noticed, but when you do "live" radio you do put yourself in the fishbowl. When you do "live" radio broadcasts your goof-ups are on display for all to hear.

I'm not making excuses, but a D. J. 's job is very busy behind the scene. Our job is to sound friendly and conversational, casually sipping a cup of coffee and spending time with you. Truth is, we are busier than a long-tailed cat in a room full of rocking chairs. While we are trying to carry an engaging and intelligent conversation, we run a control board with dozens of buttons, lights, switches and meters. All the while we watch a digital clock, timing things to the nano second. I fly airplanes and would you believe it's actually easier to fly a plane than to operate the radio control board? Honestly. Now the mistakes don't compare, of course. It's why they call it pilot *error* not *errors*. When you fly a plane, you're only allowed one serious mistake.

So with this Learjet engineer on the phone, I was wondering if I had goofed up again. However, the engineer was not angry, but amused. It turns out that Derek, a structural engineer, was actually an American Family Radio listener. He confirmed that indeed there *is* a chicken chunker and invited me to visit the plant to see how they make arguably the best jet aircraft in the world - and to actually see the chicken cannon.

I took him up on his offer. I flew to Wichita, Kansas and met Derek at the plant. It was a state-of-the-art factory. Everything was top shelf and professional. I knew I was in an important place when, at the security briefing, I was told that cameras or recording devices were not allowed inside and was instructed to fill out some paperwork. One of the first questions that reinforced my suspicions that this is serious business was, "Have you ever been convicted of espionage?"

I was given a tour and saw first-hand why the Learjet slogan for years was "Nothing else comes close." Their top-quality product is the industry standard. Finally, we made it to the launching area, I approached the cannon room with a *Raiders of the Lost Ark* wonder. There I was Indiana J. J. about to witness something few men had ever seen with their naked eye. I felt I should almost hold my breath and speak in hushed tones. I entered reverently, anxious to see that thing that few have seen and lived to tell about. Okay, maybe I did watch too much television as a kid, but this was pretty exciting!

There it was! I actually saw the cannon. And there in the yard of the shooting range were an assortment of partial wings and sundry aircraft parts revealing black eyes of simulated bouts with highflying, unfortunate fowl.

I considered filing the following report with AFR news:

Reporting live from inside the firing range, I'm J. J. Jasper with an eyewitness report (imagine newsy sounding theme music here). *I met the marksman (we'll call him Joe Cannon Shooter) and learned there is not just one operator, but several. They fire it only occasionally, not in eight-hour shifts as I supposed. They run two different kinds of tests using 4 lb. and 8 lb chickens. They purchase the chickens from just down the road (I'm not making this up). And recently they had to start using turkeys because the chickens were too small for the weight requirements.*

Last but not least, a bit of irony. I would produce a picture to prove this but was not allowed so you're just gonna have to take my word for it. If you stand directly behind the cannon and look to your right, out across the field in plain view is a KFC! *This concludes this behind the scene eyewitness report...I'm J. J. Jasper (more newsy theme music here).*

———•◦•◦•———

Chicken Tetraflingy

One medium sized chicken

One large industrial strength OSHA-approved chicken cannon

No salt or pepper necessary

Safety goggles

Pre-heat cannon to 350 degrees. Lightly grease cannon barrel. Position cannon, then stuff chicken into cannon. *Use only a qualified chicken shooter to operate cannon (one of those Chick-fil-A cows would probably gladly volunteer), then aim, shoot and serve.

No husband has ever been shot while doing the dishes.

8
MY GIRLS

A wise man once said, "If you happen upon a turtle sitting on top of a fence post, you can be sure he had help getting there."

Well, *this* little turtle has had lots of help, and many wonderful people have influenced my life. Too many, in fact, to adequately give credit to all of them. But four men who have significantly impacted my life immediately come to mind: Charles Kreisle, Oda Shouse, Steve Hallman and Randall Murphree are men who have taken me under their wing to mentor me. I will be forever grateful for the sacrifice, time, patience and dedication that these men have invested in my life in hopes that I would be all God intended me to be. I have lots to learn and a long way to go, but I want to give special thanks to these men and so many others for their love, prayers and support.

My Grandmother
The woman in my life who has probably influenced me the most is my grandmother. Blanche Gatewood-Boutcher, my Mom's mother, was born in 1911 in Yelvington, Kentucky, near Owensboro, Kentucky. Grandma was a simple woman born to poor dirt farmers. She was unassuming and uneducated. She and my grand-

father lived on a small farm. When we were very young the farm included a few pigs, chickens, a cow or two and an old mule. They had well water, no indoor plumbing, a tin roof, an apple orchard, a porch complete with a porch swing, a nice garden and a feather bed.

What wonderful experiences I had as a child, like something right out of Walton's mountain. We would eat lunch there many Sunday afternoons, and you should have seen the spread. Grandma would have lots of home cookin', garden fresh vegetables, several kinds of meat to choose from, and always a homemade dessert. And if I close my eyes, I can still hear the squeak of the porch swing chain and see that ol' No. 2 washtub hanging on the outbuilding near the barn.

Holidays there resembled a Norman Rockwell painting. We would drive out to the country to Grandma's house, and right before we reached her house, we crossed a long winding levee between two lakes. It was beautiful to see those lakes ringed with trees that gloriously changed colors with the four seasons.

My most cherished holiday memories were there at Grandma's house. Just being at Grandma's house made holidays special. Not necessarily spending the night sleeping in that big old fluffy goose down featherbed or listening to the rain falling on the tin roof or wrapped in a quilt huddled close in front of the flickering flame in the fireplace, but the love we felt from Grandma. She had an incredible capacity to love and love us unconditionally.

She also loved God with all her heart. She taught Sunday school at Yelvington Baptist for over 50 years. Grandma loved the Lord and she loved others as herself. When she wasn't taking food to someone hurting, she was sitting up with someone in the hospital. She was a precious, godly, loving servant.

Once I was working on a construction job. When the contractor of the construction site found out I was Blanche Gatewood's grandson, he pulled me over to the side and told me a story I'll never forget. He shared that, many years ago, he attended the little country church with grandma, and as a young teen he and his fiancee were about to be married. They were young, in love and dirt poor. When my grandmother found out they had no money for a wedding ring – much less anything else – the contractor told me with tears welling up in his eyes that she quietly slipped off her wedding ring and gave it to the bride to keep and to be married with.

Of course, she never told anyone. That was just one example of her life of sacrifice. That was my grandmother, a humble, loving servant who found true joy in helping others.

I moved in with her after high school and *saw* her dedication and watched her example. I loved hearing the stories of how God was faithful during the depression years. She would often tell of the old days when they had barn raisings and took in crops for others who got sick. She was *there* during the horse and buggy days. I guess my admiration is so great for my grandmother, because she knew how to love. Someone has well said, "Love is to life, what sunshine is to stained glass."

She had no wealth, no apparent influence; she barely had an eighth grade education. She never flew on an airplane or saw the ocean, and there is a long list of other things she never saw and things she didn't experience. But she was rich with love. She had mastered the art. If you paid her a visit she would light up. She had a way of making each person feel special, and like she was an honored guest just by being in their presence. She was a great listener; she cared about things you cared about.

Because of my uncle steadfastly sharing the gospel with me and my grandma *demonstrating* the love of Jesus, my life was turned around for the Lord. Grandma's prayers (she *knew* how to pray), her Christian example and her love won me to the Lord. I say this with all honesty: because of the path I was on, if it had not been for my Grandma's influence, I believe I would be dead or incarcerated today. I love her and miss her very much.

We laid her to rest in July, 2000. I wish you could have met my Grandma. I can't say enough good things about her. Oh, sure, she wasn't perfect, and she had her faults – but it's funny because I can't remember any of them. You know, come to think of it, now I understand what the Bible means in that verse that says, "Love covers a multitude of sins."

My mother

My mother, Martha Jasper, is kind, gentle, loving, patient and one of the most thoughtful people you'll ever meet. Mom is an avid reader, a threat to unsuspecting cross word puzzles and very intelligent. She was Thruston School's valedictorian.

I was probably seven or eight before I knew she was handicapped. A neighborhood boy inquired about my crippled mother. Crippled? All I knew up 'till that point was that she was the prettiest girl in the whole wide world and she was my Mama. Sure enough though, Mom is handicapped. She has a hereditary neuromuscular disorder that primarily affects the feet, legs and hands. It is a severe form of muscular atrophy. Mom struggles to walk and has limited use of her hands.

I guess I never realized it, however, because she worked 40 hours a week, raised all four kids – "stair-steps," we were all born within six years – and *never* complained. My mother has had a difficult life with many obstacles, but she never let her handicap prevent her from doing anything. Strong, resilient and brave, my mother is a survivor.

She is wonderful, but like most sons I don't tell her or show her often enough. Once I cooked up a little surprise to hopefully make her feel extra special. It was a Mother's Day weekend, and I was planning to fly home and surprise her and take her out to eat. I sent a Mother's Day card early so it would arrive on Friday or Saturday.

I had told her I had a weekend commitment, and I called on Saturday to wish her Happy Mother's Day. I told her I was calling on Saturday in case I was out of pocket and didn't get to call her on Sunday.

"Thank you sweetheart," she said. "I got your lovely card."

Well, little did she know that I was calling from the airport and about to board a flight to come home, surprise her and take her out to eat. I had already called my sister and arranged for her to invite Mom to dinner at the nicest restaurant in town.

After arriving in Owensboro, Kentucky, I started putting the surprise in motion. I paid an early visit to The Moonlight, *the* barbeque restaurant in town, where later that night my sister would be bringing Mom. I asked the restaurant manager if I could come back to the restaurant and wear a disguise and actually be Mom's waiter. I explained I wanted to surprise my Mother.

They graciously agreed, and so next I got with friends who had stopped by a costume shop and purchased some elaborate makeup. Temporary black hair dye, full, real-looking eyebrows, a mustache that would have made Groucho Marx proud – the works.

I returned to the restaurant after my makeover. At first the manager didn't recognize me. My blonde hair was now black and pulled back in a ponytail, not to mention the big black bushy eyebrows, mustache and sunglasses. But after explaining who I was, they allowed me to dress in waiter attire.

Mom showed up as planned. I had already cautioned my sister to do all the talking. I basically walked up with pen and pad in hand, poured water and tried to stay over Mom's shoulder so she couldn't get a good look at me. This went on for a while – in fact, all through dinner. I kept refilling their glasses and taking plates away.

I had never worked in a restaurant, so the waitresses and waiters were giving me cues on when to go and what to do. This started getting fun for everyone because the other waiters were telling the customers at the other tables, "See that fella, he is a D. J. from Mississippi, that's his mom and he really has blonde hair. He wants to provide a Mother's Day surprise."

Well, a log jam occurred at the restaurant, because no one wanted to leave! They wanted to witness the end result. I decided I'd better make my move. I went to the table just as my mother was telling my sister how she missed me and wished I lived closer. I revealed myself at that exact moment, Mom was shocked, placed her hands on her mouth, and cried – while the other patrons applauded. It had the makings of an old black-and-white movie. You almost felt as if Jimmy Stewart should be entering the room at any time.

My mother doesn't get enough excitement in her life. I wanted to surprise her to help her feel like a queen for the day. I have a great mom…how do you say thanks to the one who carried you for nine months, changed your diapers, sat up rocking you when you were sick, cooked and cleaned and hauled you around like a taxi service, and all the many other thankless things moms do? Thanks again, Mom, you're the best. You exemplify all that is good about the word "Mom."

My Mother-in-Law

My mother-in-law, Kandi Anderson, was born in South Texas and now resides in Gulfport, Mississippi. Kandi is a talented radio broadcaster – she works with American Family Radio network station WAOY on the Mississippi Gulf Coast – and newspaper columnist. She has movie star good looks (she looks half her age and actually did some modeling in her teen years), a bubbly morning show personality and the compassion of Mother Teresa. Those of you who know Kandi know I'm not exaggerating. Quite a combination, huh? She has many reasons to boast, but you'll not find a more humble servant.

Kandi absolutely adores Lowry, her husband of nearly 30 years. She loves the Lord, and is devoted to her children and grandchildren. She is a very talented writer and a popular conference speaker.

However, she has absolutely ruined my opportunity to tell standard mother-in-law jokes, because she *is* a near-perfect mother-in-law. Kandi treats me like a son and I love her like a mother. In my opinion, her crowning achievement was giving birth to and raising the best of her three children, Melanie, whom I chose to have and to hold. Wow, I've scored enough points here to keep me in good graces 'til the cows come home!

My Wife

I have real concerns about my wife, Melanie, going to heaven. She is so incredibly sweet and kind that I'm afraid she'll zoom way past it!

I met Melanie through her mother, Kandi. When introduced to Melanie, I came down with a full-blown case of "love at first sight" syndrome. Melanie is gorgeous, godly and absolutely the best wife and mother I could hope for. She is a tremendous athlete, a strong supportive "behind the scenes" type and is very talented in many ways. She works hard at her career as a pre-adolescent training and development coordinator (stay-at-home-mom). Everything Melanie attempts she excels at. Shortly after we married, we purchased a lakefront lot, fulfilling a life long dream for us both. When we prayerfully decided to build a home, Mel actually drew up the plans. She has no background in architecture or construction; she's just a show-me-one-time-and-I-can-do-it kind of gal.

We started clearing trees, digging, pouring concrete footings and laying foundation blocks. We started in January, and our target date for completion was Thanksgiving. I reassured her, "Honey, trust me, we'll be completely moved in and celebrate Thanksgiving in our new home."

(*Editor's note: The Jaspers spent Thanksgiving Day laying concrete blocks for the fireplace, and Thanksgiving dinner was take-out from a hotel restaurant. In drizzling rain, both suffering from colds, Mel mixed mortar and carried block while J. J. laid them. Mel was overheard to say, "I WILL NOT work Christmas Day – that's were I draw the line!" J. J. was rumored to have asked, "How about a half day on Christmas?")

Currently the cabin is 90% complete. We are grateful to God for the most difficult and most rewarding project (aside from parenting) we've ever tackled. My Renaissance wife, along with many precious friends and family, built an entire house during evenings after work and on weekends. Mel gave my ego quite a bruising by working harder, longer hours and accomplishing more than I did. And I have a construction background, while she had zero experience. Basically, I helped her build the cabin where we now live and call home.

There is not a sweeter, kinder, more caring person on earth, but her greatest gift is compassion. Oh, she's got a feisty side for sure, but you'll not meet a more gentle, loving person. I don't let a day go by without thanking God for allowing me to have my best friend as a wife.

Lauren

Our daughter, Lauren, is the main attraction at our house. I think the name Lauren in the original Greek means, "Lil' tornado." She fills everyday with a few breaks, a few spills, a few tears, but mostly a lot of joy and laughter. She provides lots of adventure and excitement and she has probably already taught me more than I'll ever teach her.

We once bought her a yellow Labrador Retriever puppy for her birthday. She named him Chief. One night, I quietly opened her bedroom door and peeked in to check on her. She had taken off all her clothes and dressed chief in them and she lay sound asleep without a stitch of clothes on! I didn't know dogs could blush, but I think when I looked into his big brown eyes, clad with Lauren's too-tight pajamas, he was a rather embarrassed puppy.

Lauren's first pet was a fish. She had pestered mom about a pet for so long, that Mel gave in. She thought long and hard about the most low-maintenance pet on the planet and finally purchased a fish in a plastic bag of water. No deluxe aquarium with all the bells, whistles and bubbles. No, this little survivor was going to have to fend for himself in the old fashioned fish bowl.

On the way home from the pet store, after Mel gave her the old "It's your pet and you're going to have to be responsible for him" speech, she asked Lauren if she had thought of a name.

"No, not really," Lauren said.

"Well, since this is your very own pet, you get to decide. You name the fish, honey, it's yours to name," Mel said, prodding her on. Then she asked again, "What do you want to call him?"

After a moment, Lauren cheerfully declared, "Don Wildmon."

"Don Wildmon?" Mel repeated. "You're going to name your fish Don Wildmon?"

Lauren laughed out loud, patted Mel's leg and said with a twinkle in her eye, "I'm just joking." A three-year-old making a joke and delivering the punch line with expert timing – that's my girl! (We'll have her behind a control board wearing headphones in no time.)

Lauren attends a wonderful Christian school, Lakeview Baptist Academy, run by Pastor Robert Garland. Her teacher, Mrs. Lora Garland, is such a blessing. The Garlands are a precious couple and a joy to be around. God has given them such a wonderful gift of working with and ministering to children. At Lauren's K-4 graduation, she received all the awards she could possibly win, except for two. She absolutely loves school and we highly recommend Christian education.

She is an exceptionally bright girl, but we were suspect

about her tales of tutoring some of the other students out in the hallway. We quizzed her teacher, who acknowledged that indeed, Lauren was finishing her work early and showing an aptitude for helping the other students with their reading. Our four-year-old was already tutoring!

We asked Lauren if they placed her and the other students in the hall so they wouldn't distract the class. "Of course not," she declared. "They put us in the hall so the other students wouldn't distract us!"

With our Lauren there is no shortage of confidence or creativity. Lauren is a fun, bright, talented little blessing and loves Jesus Christ with her whole heart – and will tell you so!

Sadie

Mel and I were faithfully praying for a baby, but Lauren was the best little prayer warrior of all. Nearly every single day, she would stop in the middle of playing with her toys and dolls, clasp her chubby little hands together, and pray for a little sister.

She grew impatient. *We* grew impatient. "When is God going to answer my prayer and send us a baby from heaven?" she would ask.

After several years, we wondered if there were medical complications. One night at a home Bible study, in which several of the families were expecting babies, they asked light-heartedly when we were going to "get with the program."We had close friends and family praying earnestly with us, but hadn't said much at Bible study. We shared our desires and concerns. We had had our hopes up for so many months just to be continually disappointed; and now all the questions and fears were settling in.

One of the men suggested we sit in chairs, and invited

the others to gather around us and lay hands on us and pray, as it instructs in James 5. After that very special time of prayer from our precious bible study cell group, we had a breakthrough. The *very* next month, I came home and there in the kitchen was my wife, barefoot and expecting!

Our little answered prayer, Sadie Morgan, was born March 14, 2001. She is perfect. We marvel at God's miracle-working, life-giving capacity. Newborns bring so much joy. The way they look, feel and that sweet unmistakable baby smell is second to none.

Melanie and I have always been strongly pro-life, but there's nothing quite like actually being in the delivery room and watching a baby being born to reinforce your belief in the sanctity of human life. Taking part in that process makes me even more certain that *all* life is sacred and we should strive to protect our innocent ones. Every child is precious in the sight of God and they should be precious to us.

And Sadie *is* precious, however, it is a little too soon to tell exactly what her personality is like! But in the eating, sleeping, crying and sewage department, she gets straight A's. She's a true blessing. We've decided we're gonna keep her!

Five out of four people have trouble with fractions.

9

BED AND BREAKFAST

Have you ever stayed at a bed and breakfast? It's a pretty novel idea how someone takes an old home, rich with history and converts it into room and board for a night. Antiques and collectibles usually grace the rooms. Pictures in the hallway often help tell the story behind these mansions or old home places. You find yourself slowly meandering about, reflecting on the people and their time period and wishing "if only these walls could talk." Any uneasiness with sharing a bathroom with the other guests or gathering around a table with strangers for meals is countered by the unique atmosphere and wonderful experience of a bed and breakfast. The trade offs from conventional lodging are usually well worth it.

Once I spent the night in Pampa, Texas at the Hughey House Bed and Breakfast. The 5,500 square foot home was built by I. B. Hughey for his family in 1926. The Hughey House was Pampa's first bed and breakfast. Much of its original furniture and features remain after over 70 years and it maintains an elegance and warmth in one of the Texas panhandle's oldest homes.

I also stayed in a "castle" in the mountains of West Virginia one weekend. Poised on a hillside above the small mountain town of Elkins, the majestic Graceland mansion commands a 20 mile view of the beautiful Tygart Valley. When Senator Henry Davis built this extravagant summer home in 1893 he named it for his fifth child, Grace – hence the name Graceland (not to be confused with Memphis, thank you very much). Its turreted, Queen Anne architecture blends native oak, cherry and maple timbers with Tiffany glass, and a broad, imposing stairway, lending a country elegance to the rustic castle.

Once my wife Melanie and I stayed in a musty, creepy old turn-of-the-century bed and breakfast that would have served as a perfect cure for someone suffering from narcolepsy. Too many squeaks, too many shadows. It was a long night and a quick lesson in eeriness. Not a good recipe for a good night's sleep. Next time you camp out, give me a call and I'll come over, crawl in the tent and tell you the whole spooky story with a flashlight, real late at night.

Last year I was scheduled to be the entertainment/ speaker for a banquet at Mennonite Brethren Church in Buhler, Kansas. Arrangements had been made well in advance and reservations were made for me to stay in a bed and breakfast. After an uneventful flight, I was shuttled to Buhler where the pastor's wife picked me up and took me to my lodging.

To my surprise we pulled into the parking lot of The Sunshine Meadows Retirement Community. "We're here," she declared. Of course I thought she was joking and laughed. She got a funny look on her face, and appeared a bit uncomfortable. "Here we are," she said. I smiled politely, still convinced she was pulling my leg. "Well," she continued, "Here we go."

I finally broke my silence and declared, "This is a rest home!"

"Oh, no," she said with obvious embarrassment. "We should have called to explain. Buhler is so small we have no hotel or motel, so the folks here at Sunshine Meadows, graciously allow us to have a room for guests. This *IS* our bed and breakfast!"

"Get outta here! You've got to be kidding!" I said, still considering the possibility of a prank. I thought, *she's either joking and this is some academy award winning acting job, or she's serious and they are actually putting me up in an old folks home and calling it a bed and breakfast!* It was no joke. I unloaded the luggage, went to the room and sure enough as plain as your teeth in a glass, there on the door was the sign marked "Guests." Now, anyone who knows me knows I love and respect senior citizens. But the sights and sounds of a nursing home are unmistakable. The layout was standard – the sights, sounds, etc…confirmed we were at a nursing home. I expected any minute to hear the cries of, "Help me, help me!" wafting down the hall like meows of a kitten trapped in a tree. I attempted to call my wife and let her know that I had arrived safely, only to discover there was *no* phone.

After a long flight and drive, I immediately journeyed to the restroom, which looked like it was designed by NASA. There were handlebars, foot petals and safety rails. There was even a call button so in case I accidentally fell down I could notify the front desk of my plight.

Imagine all of the questions going through my mind. Are they going to wake me at 3 a. m. to check my blood pressure? Will someone be coming in to roll me over and give me a shot or worse!? Could I escape if I had to?

That night at the banquet during the meal the pastor

had fun quizzing me about the bed and breakfast accommodations. Not wanting to appear ungrateful I said, "It's nice, but yes, I was indeed surprised." The pastor enjoyed a good laugh and said he had tried to convince his wife to book a hotel in the larger neighboring town. I assured him I wouldn't mention it from the stage.

"No," he insisted, "You really should. We should know better than to invite a stand-up comedian and put him up in a nursing home and expect him not to mention it. I think you should. No, I *want* you to. Come out of the chute with it. Milk it for all it's worth. Get all the mileage you can out of it."

I took his advice and described my accommodations to the audience. Oh, I assured them, I'm not too good to stay there. "Hey, I'm a Kentucky boy living in Mississippi. I can easily sleep in the back seat of a car – and have!

But I told them the element of surprise did throw me off balance. Plus I was concerned about serious travelers who decide to buy a travel directory and make plans to travel the country staying in bed and breakfasts. They'll go to the eastern seaboard and maybe stay in a converted lighthouse or travel down south and stay in an old antebellum home.

"Listen, when they arrive in Buhler, Kansas and see what you folks call a bed and breakfast, it's gonna take the meaning of the word surprise to a whole new level," I said. "I mean, bed and *breakfast* – I don't even want to know about the breakfast," I deadpanned. "I get enough bran and I don't like prunes! Keep the breakfast. I've only been in Buhler a couple of hours and I've already had enough surprises. Maybe it's irony or God's fun way to humble me, but last night I was in L. A. staying in the Hilton Hotel and tonight I'm in Buhler and you've put me in a nursing home!!!"

Concluding my near manic delivery about my lodging, I ended the good-natured tirade with this conclusion: "I'm not making this up. I would invite you all to my room to see for yourselves, but I'm not allowed visitors after 8:00 p.m.!" The crowd roared with delight. They were a great audience with a wonderful sense of humor.

Oh, to their credit, the Sunshine Meadows Retirement Community is more of an assisted-living facility than a nursing home. It's professional, upscale and very nice. Check it out for yourself. If you're ever in Buhler, Kansas, and need a good, clean reasonably priced room to stay in, visit Sunshine Meadows. They'll leave a light on for ya. Tell 'em J. J. sent you.

———•◦•———

Shocks and surprises are part of life – they will come. A sense of humor is a good way to deal with the curves life throws us. We sometimes laugh lest we cry. Putting on the "full armor" as mentioned in Ephesians 6, is another way.

Humble yourselves before the Lord, and he will lift you up (James 4: 10). God gives us the privilege to *humble* ourselves. He opposes the proud. If we don't choose wisely and remain humble, God has lots of creative ways to keep us humble. A haughty spirit comes before a fall.

Q: What is E.T. short for?
A: Because he has little legs.

10
HUMOR

Bob Vila is coming out with a new TV show about middle-aged couples that have had plastic surgery. It's called *This Old Spouse*.

Did that make you laugh? I hope so, because I love to laugh and I enjoy making people laugh. Laughter, especially from children, is absolute music to my ears. I believe we should all laugh more than we do. Laughter is to life what shock absorbers are to a car. It doesn't take the potholes out of the road, but it sure makes the ride easier.

Do you know what Winnie the Pooh and John the Baptist have in common? They both liked honey and they both have the same middle name. See, that grin looks good on you. Someone has well said, "You're never fully dressed without a smile."

Did you hear about the man who bought his wife a mood ring? She said, "When I'm in a good mood it turns blue, and when I'm in a bad mood it leaves a red mark on his forehead!"

Humor has been an important part of my life. I was branded the cut-up in my family and the class clown in school. I began my broadcasting career in 1985, and most of my listeners over the years have said that encouragement and humor are my on-air signature. Before broadcasting I was involved in youth ministry, where you have to have a sense of humor to survive. Years of public speaking taught me the importance of humor as an icebreaker to help remove barriers and open an avenue of communication. It's easier to slip an important message into a funny illustration and use that "spoonful of sugar to help the medicine go down."

My day job is being a weekday morning on-air personality at American Family Radio, but weekends stay busy with public speaking events and doing stand-up comedy at banquets, fairs, fundraisers, etc. In 1996 I even recorded a comedy video, *J. J. Jasper World Tour – One Night Only!*

Since laughter is such a huge part of who I am, morning listeners to American Family Radio have to endure a steady diet of lame jokes, one liners and lots of *pun*-ishment between songs. If it's any consolation to you, I know those jokes are really corny! But whether you laugh or moan I don't care – I'm just trying to get some kind of reaction from you, to brighten your day. (And you'd be surprised what you can get away with early in the morning.)

Yes, I'm convinced everyone everywhere needs a good laugh occasionally. Laughter is a universal language and a universal need. We are way too stressed out, worried, rushed and depressed. They say you can tell a lot about people by the way they handle traffic jams, lost luggage and tangled Christmas lights. Life *is* serious but sometimes we need to take our situation and ourselves a little less seriously.

Once when our daughter, Lauren, was still a toddler, we were at home getting ready to go out. Melanie and Lauren got in the car, but I was running late. It had been *one of those days*. And I had been a royal pain – a real grouch.

After I climbed in, closed the door and buckled up, Lauren said in her childlike way, "Daddy, Mommy said not to mention it, but she said you were mad at the world! Well, I wanna know, how can you be mad at every single person in the whole wide world – and why would you want to be?" Sometimes you really do have to laugh to keep from crying.

On several occasions I've been invited to retreats to teach on the benefits of humor. If you will allow me, I'd like to share some of my notes with you.

Laughter is Healthy

Did you know that laughter is essential to our equilibrium and to our well-being? If we're not well, laughter helps us get well; if we are well, laughter helps us stay that way. It increases our immunity to infections by instantly increasing a flood of disease-fighting cells and proteins into the blood. Studies show frequent laughter helps lower blood pressure, relieve stress and control pain.

Laughing is also aerobic, providing a workout for the diaphragm and increasing the body's ability to utilize oxygen. One laugh burns six calories and laughing heartily 100 times a day has the same benefit as ten minutes on a rowing machine. (Wow, no more going to the gym! Now you can just sit at home in that favorite chair and laugh the pounds away. Sure, people will think you're crazy, but you'll live longer and healthier. Then who'll be laughing?)

It's no wonder that some hospitals and companies now have humor workshops and seminars. More and more professionals are realizing the benefits of laughter.

Sure, some diseases may be contagious, but none is as contagious as the cure – laughter.

Hey this just dawned on me. I'm not sure just how much you paid for this book or if you feel you got your money's worth, but if you add in the registration cost of a seminar…Wow, I'm way ahead here. You may even owe me more money! If this is years from now and you've purchased this at a yard sale for 10 cents, you got a real steal!

So go ahead, consider it sound medical advice to indulge in the luxury of laughter.

Laughter is Beneficial

Laughter helps cut our troubles down to a size we can deal with.

Laughter makes precious memories. It's usually those hilarious times when you've laughed the hardest that you remember the most. Can you remember your fondest holiday memories? A funny incident probably occurred to make it a favorite.

Laughing at ourselves breaks down barriers between others and us. It makes us seem more approachable. Laughter is like a magnet that attracts people. If you really want to know someone, just watch him or her laugh.

Laughter is even profitable. The advertising geniuses on Madison Avenue have learned that the fastest route to the viewer's heart runs smack dab through the funny bone. Year after year, the top ads ranked by Ad Meter (in the magazine *Advertising Age*) have all been humorous ones. (Remember those Super Bowl ads?) And look at people like Jerry Seinfeld, Jeff Foxworthy, Mark Lowrey and the late Jerry Clower – they all made laughter and humor into a career.

Laughter is Biblical

It is scriptural to laugh and be joyful. Ecclesiastes 3: 4 says, "There is a time to weep and a time to laugh," and all through the Psalms David spoke of making a joyful noise to the Lord. Joy is everywhere in the bible: "Shout joyfully to the Lord, all the earth," (Psalm 98: 4 KJV); "Make a joyful noise unto the Lord, all ye lands! Serve the Lord with gladness," (Psalm 100: 1-2 KJV); "Then our mouth was filled with laughter, and our tongue with singing," (Psalm 126: 2 KJV).

I believe laughter is a God-given gift that we should treasure. It is one of the secrets to a long and enjoyable life. We as adults have lost sight of that. The sad fact is that children, on average, laugh about 400 times a day, while adults only laugh about 15 times. Why did 385 laughs disappear? People don't stop laughing because they grow old. They grow old because they stop laughing. God intended us to use humor and laughter to bring joy to others. (If you doubt that God has a sense of humor, look in the mirror.)

Even though laughter is healthy, beneficial and perhaps most of all, Biblical, trying to figure out how to make people laugh is no joke!

Have you ever thought about how difficult it is to do stand-up comedy? Most people are afraid to speak in front of crowds, much less try to make them laugh. Can you imagine how difficult it is to be funny after traveling all day on a plane, maybe after losing your luggage or having had a fight with your wife before you left home? Thankfully, I enjoy it and it comes easily. However, stand-up comedy can be brutal.

Believe me there is a big difference between getting on a roll at a party with friends when you feel funny and you're in a great mood, and having to stand before a crowd who's thinking, *Be funny, I dare you.* In their minds they're going, *3-2-1 Go! Make me laugh.*

What puts so much pressure on you is the fact that you are graded right on the spot. Think about it – a singer can miss a note and a preacher can have a sermon fall a little flat, and not realize whether or not the audience noticed. Stand-up comedy is unique because, if it's good people are laughing, and the better it is the harder the audience laughs. But if it's not funny you find out fast – it's like having the teacher grade your papers right in front of you.

I've been amused to notice over the years that when you're telling a joke or funny story to a friend on the job, you basically only get two reactions. If the joke is funny, they laugh. If it's not, they say with raised eyebrows, "Oh, that's funny!" Check it out, next time you're around the water cooler telling a really good one. "Hey, do you know what a snail says riding on a turtle's back? WHEE!!!" Okay, did you laugh just now, or say, *"Oh, that's funny!"*

Then to make the job more difficult is that, if people aren't laughing right at first, you can quickly go south and bomb altogether. For a D. J. the biggest fear is what's known as dead air. The biggest fear for a comic is little or no laughter – or you start to get those nervous "courtesy laughs."

I was in front of a huge crowd once in Cincinnati, and things started out badly. So I began to try harder (which is like over compensating when you're driving in the snow, and try too hard to correct a slide.) and that just makes matters worse – a comedian must stay calm! If your face turns red and Lord forbid you get nervous, the crowd will sense it. Dobermans, small children and audiences have a sixth sense about fear when you begin to panic.

There I was, struggling in Cincinnati and no one was laughing. My face was hot and burning. Instead of taking a deep breath and regaining my composure, I tried harder and harder. (Thankfully, there were no hecklers.) I was flying it into the ground. Are you getting nervous *for* me? My palms have started to sweat all over again. I was sliding on that snowy road. What started out as a simple fishtail, ended up with me spinning wildly out of control and careening over the guardrail and down the cliff. If you were in Cincinnati that night or at the county fair that afternoon in Illinois – I'm sorry you didn't get your money's worth.

I've only bombed a handful of times during a ten-year comedy career, but when there's not a back-up band and it's just you, the spot light, a wooden stool and a lonely mike and you go down in flames, it's an experience you don't soon forget. (P. S. The promoter of the event doesn't forget either.)

While making people laugh is not easy, I can't stop trying. You see, I've learned a secret about you. You occasionally need a good laugh. There's a central theme in most of the mail I receive. "Thank you for cheering me up in the mornings." "Thank you for making me laugh."

Please don't get me wrong – I know you can go too far with humor. The Bible warns against idle words and coarse joking. There are many situations where laughter is not appropriate.

And, of course, humor should be G-rated. That's why I'm not a big fan of modern-day comedians. In my opinion today's popular comedians attempt to shock people off of their chairs in an effort to buy a cheap laugh or two. Their brand of humor requires little effort or talent and is inappropriate and in poor taste. Give me the old classics. The longevity of the "I Love Lucy" type of comedy dispels the myth that it has to be dirty to be funny. You remember when the best humor was the good, clean kind? It still is!

Despite the potential pitfalls in comedy, however, I still think laughter is incredibly important. As a Christian stand-up comedian, I've witnessed people laugh until tears streamed down their faces. I've had to wade through the laughter to continue to the next funny story. On many occasions, people seek me out after a banquet to say, "Thank you. I haven't laughed this hard in weeks or months." They say, "Thank you, I needed that."

I've attempted to make a case for humor and laughter in this chapter – I'm not trying to convert you into a court jester or advocate foolishness. I'm simply trying to remind you that laughter is the brush that sweeps the cobwebs from our lives. Sometimes we do need to lighten up, not be so sour – give ourselves permission to laugh. Life is hard, but we don't have to always be so pious and somber that we're afraid to smile. Sometimes we have to look for the humor in a difficult situation.

One reason I stayed away from church as a boy was all of the frowns I observed. The only church people I knew had faces so long they could've sucked golf balls out of gopher holes. They looked like they had been baptized in lemon juice. Now, as a born-again, baptized, spirit-filled believer in Jesus Christ, I know without a doubt, there's joy in the journey!

———

Is your faith attractive? Your attitude is contagious – is it worth catching? With our whole hearts let's believe and live the principle expressed in Proverbs 17: 22, "A merry heart does good like a medicine."

You know why cannibals don't eat clowns?
They taste funny.

11
MISTLETOE

It's called feast or famine. Unless you've been a construction worker you can't fully appreciate the difference between summer income and winter income.

Usually, spring and summer months are favorable weather-wise, and you can get lots of work done. When old man winter flexes his muscles, however, it's a different story. Ice, snow and freezing temperatures prevent most outdoor work. Steak in the summer and bologna (we called it "Jasper steak" growing up) in the winter. Oh, sure, you could make Larry Burkett proud, save, budget and store up for winter, but that would be un-American.

Kenny and I were in our twenties, best friends living in Kentucky and working together as brick masons. Sometimes winters in Kentucky could be brutal. One winter was particularly mean, with paralyzing cold and a lot of snow. Construction work ground to a halt. Fortunately for me, I had just moved to the much warmer, Mississippi. Kenny was already starting to suffer from cabin fever and called from Kentucky to say he would really like to come for a visit since the forced lay-off, but should probably stick around and hunt some temporary work.

"Come on down," I said. "I've been thinking of a plan on how to make a lot of money quick – and I've got a great idea." (A word of advice here…stand back when you hear phrases like "Get rich quick" or "This can't fail" or "Don't worry, it's strong enough to hold us both" or "It's okay I've seen it done on TV" and especially if they include the name Bubba – take cover quickly!)

I had a plan that *couldn't* fail and we were young and dumb – all the makings of a pretty volatile combination. Kenny bought a seventy-five dollar car to make the trip. He wanted to leave the reliable vehicle with his wife and daughters and he explained how the car purchase was cheaper than the bus or airfare, and assured me he had gotten a bargain. He said he'd see me in six hours.

Kenny called me from Columbia, Tennessee. The wheel had fallen off his seventy-five dollar car…imagine that. You know they just don't make 'em like they used to. Kenny once bought a Chevy pick-up with a *Buick* motor in it. Don't ask me – I have no idea. My guess is a little bit of creativity and a whole lot of parts left over! Have you ever noticed how it takes a lot more time and nearly as much cash to jerry-rig something? Not to mention all the head-aches. But it seems we never learn and we keep trying to pound that square peg in a round hole, thinking we're getting a deal.

Well, the car was traveling one way and the prodigal wheel took off in a different direction. Actually, to hear Kenny tell it, the car skidded to a halt with a bone jarring thud and the wheel kept rolling and bouncing down the road. More free advice: if you insist on driving seventy-five dollar cars, buy insurance coverage from Lloyds of London or at least maintain a good sense of humor. Good-natured Kenny has the latter. He took it all in stride, managed to get the car up on all fours and continued south on course.

Meanwhile my *great plan* was for us to *sell mistletoe* during the Christmas holidays. (In case you've never heard of this fun Christmas tradition, some people hang it in a doorway and stand under it and steal a kiss from their sweetheart.)

Mistletoe grows plentifully in the tops of large oak trees. When we were pretty small, Dad would use a shotgun to blast the mistletoe from trees. We would gather the mistletoe, separate it into small bunches, tie a red ribbon around each sprig and head downtown to sell it.

There were no malls when I was very young, so downtown at Christmastime bustled like the first hour of a yard sale. We would stand on a street corner to sell our wares to Christmas shoppers all the while praying that none of our grade school classmates would happen by. The difference between embarrassment and absolute humiliation is if the prettiest girl or most popular boy walks up while you're doing something you feel is ridiculous. In later years, my brother tried the same method and actually sold over five hundred dollars worth of mistletoe in just a couple of evenings. (I know, "Really! Wow!" was my reaction too!)

I told Kenny the story and he pointed out that my brother used his adorable small-too-hard-to-resist children as salespersons and we were grown men for crying out loud.

"Trust me, Kenny, this is gonna work," I insisted. Besides we were flat broke. I hope you can relate to being economically challenged – I hope I'm not the only one who, during hardtimes experienced the absolute thrill of finding loose change between the cushions of the couch after much scrounging. Grandma used to say, "Being poor ain't a sin, but it can sure be mighty inconvenient."

I had located the best mistletoe-laden tree. Because of my experience as a tree surgeon, I already owned the necessary climbing gear. I put on the climbing spikes and fastened the safety harness and started the long climb to the top of the huge oak tree. It's precarious in the uppermost limbs so I gingerly started snapping off and throwing down the mistletoe.

After many bushels, Kenny insisted we had more than enough, shouting, "You only need a small sprig per bag."

I looked all around and all I could see were dollar signs. Who said money doesn't grow on trees? I couldn't seem to quit. I hated the thought of leaving money on the tree. "Just one more minute, just one more clump," I replied. With the fervor of a California gold miner, I knew I should, but I just couldn't quit.

After Kenny's coaxing turned to threats, I finally came down. (Talk about an idle threat! What was he gonna do, climb up there and get me?) We had a long wheelbase pickup truck piled completely full. It was heaped up and rounded off.

Now we needed to find a production facility to process our product. My friend Randall lived nearby, so we commandeered his kitchen, abruptly cleared off his dining table and set up shop – to which we will hereafter refer to, as the central processing distribution center.

Let me tell you about Randall. He is one of my dearest friends. He is dignified and sophisticated. He is a former high school and college English teacher and one of the nicest people you'll ever meet. He sports a neatly trimmed gray beard and looks the part of an English butler. If you look up the word "gentleman" in the dictionary, you'll likely find Randall's picture there. Randall agreed to loan us his kitchen – I mean central processing distribution center – just so he could watch the show. It was really cheap entertainment.

The trick to making this project work, for those of you who *do* plan to try this at home, is to take a sprig, tie a red ribbon around it and put it in a plastic sandwich baggie. Of course, you have to make sure there are a couple of berries on the twig in each bag. This is very important if you want to get the right holiday look. It's actually best to put the stuff in the fridge to fog up the bag and keep it fresh, but I'm spending way too much time describing the process. Just be sure to send for my instructional mistletoe sales video – it is not available in stores anywhere.

We were racing the clock. We were losing valuable time among the Christmas shoppers. With the urgency of a Nascar pit crew, we were stuffing and tying as fast as we could. Randall was enjoying the side show, and finally volunteered to help, all the while insisting that we not pay him and demanding that we tell no one he was involved in any way. He had already made sure all the blinds were closed. I wouldn't think of mentioning Randall Murphree's name or suggesting that Randall Murphree took part in our shenanigans. Randall Murphree is too good of a friend. I totally respect Randall Murphree's wishes, so please just leave Randall Murphree out of this.

Kenny still had his doubts, but finally came around and caught my vision. Before long he started inquiring, "What are we gonna put all the money in?" We had baskets to carry the product, a card table to set up for the mistletoe and a poster with the price – but nothing to put *all* of our money in. "We need a bank bag or maybe a big satchel," Kenny said. Every ten minutes or so, as we frantically bagged mistletoe, Kenny would pipe up again, saying, "Come on you guys, you still haven't answered me. What are we gonna put the money in? We're maybe talking about lots and lots of money here."

Funny how a project, any project, can start with reservations and trepidation. You gather a small crowd, throw a sanguine personality into the mix, and it becomes an auction of enthusiasm. In just a few pep talks, it escalates quickly from, "I don't think this will work," to, "We're gonna be rich." Before Kenny and I hit the streets for the first time, we were planning franchises, and hiring district and regional managers. Folks could have salespeople down line from them, who had people down line from them – and our top sellers could win green Cadillacs to drive. We were wondering who among our friends and family would be suited to run our overseas operation.

Kenny the skeptic now had dollar signs in his eyes and was asking about the money bags so often that he had Randall in tears from laughing so hard. We were running out of daylight, but the "what ifs" drove us to bag some more and not dare leave any money sitting on Randall's table.

Finally we finished, then loaded up and headed for Wal-Mart. But Kenny's enthusiasm started to fade. "This is dumb," he said, "I feel like a total idiot."

"Put on your game face," I said. "We won't see anyone we know. This will work. Trust me."

We found a place alongside the other sidewalk holiday vendors, who were selling Christmas knick-knacks and baked goods for churches and charities.

Kenny suggested we ask permission to sell in front of Wal-Mart. I opted for the, "Easier to get forgiveness than ask permission" method. We set up the card table and began unloading the stuff.

A man approached. "Whatcha got?" he asked.

"Mistletoe," we answered.

"Great. How much?"

"One dollar." Our first customer, and we weren't even unloaded! *Wow*, I thought, *this is better than expected. The plan was working already!*

Just then a very friendly representative of Wal-Mart approached, smiling and inquiring who we were with.

"We're just with ourselves," Kenny said, "We're just trying to make a little Christmas money."

The man politely told us we could not stay there with the legitimate sidewalk vendors, who had already obtained permission.

Kenny later confessed that he'd wanted to respond to the question, "Who are you with?" by saying, "We're with the Jasper and Kessinger Foundation," knowing that this would no doubt give us a free pass. But his Christian convictions wouldn't allow it. I've always admired his high standards. We were ejected from Wal-Mart – the umpire had thrown us out of the game.

Plan B was to head to a major grocery store and hopefully sell it wholesale to the store so they could put it in the check out lane next to the cashier. Walking across the parking lot up to the store, an obviously very wealthy woman – dressed to the nine's – approached Kenny. She noticed the large full wicker baskets we were carrying and inquired what we had for sale.

Kenny mustered a meekly enthusiastic, "Mistletoe."

The woman erupted with laughter. She was not laughing with us, she was laughing at us, and there *is* a difference. Kenny threw a hand in the air and said, "That does it, that's the last straw. Let's go, I'm out of the mistletoe business."

My pleas fell on deaf ears, because Kenny was down for the count. With his ego against the ropes all evening, the woman had delivered the knockout punch.

We had synchronized our watches so we could meet

Randall at a friend's restaurant to share our success. Actually, over Randall's objections, Kenny and I insisted that we would buy Randall's supper and make him a third partner, because he sacrificed an entire Saturday to help us. (Of course, in our zeal we never got so carried away as to discuss benefits or a 401k. We were just going to pay him a handsome sum and we hoped he would be pleasantly surprised. Boy, that plan went down the tubes like all of our others.)

We entered Taco Hut with our tails between our legs. Randall and our friend Jamie Finley, the store manager, were eager to hear about our sales victory. "One dollar, only one lousy dollar," we said sadly.

Jamie and Randall were laughing uncontrollably. I think they were laughing with us, not at us, but at that point we failed to see the humor. We had worked 10 hours and spent money on bags, ribbon, gas, etc. I risked my life climbing a huge tree and we were humiliated to boot. We felt rejected and foolish, and we were taking this pretty hard. We had blown an entire Saturday. If this day had been a fish, we'd have thrown it back! Or like I've heard you ladies say, "Some days are a total waste of makeup." It seems everyone involved got a good laugh but us. We still didn't see one redeemable thing about this no-good-rotten-wasted-day. Deep down we knew one day we'd probably laugh about this, but right now our egos were stinging.

Years later, some friends bought us a "Best Mistletoe Salesmen Award" plaque from the trophy shop. Have you ever noticed some things are harder to live down than others? And just think, if I feel comfortable sharing *this* story with you, can you even imagine all of the weird, wacky, lame-brained, half-baked stunts I've been involved in that I would be *too* embarrassed to tell!

I racked my brain, trying to find a moral to this story or offer an application for living, but I kept coming up empty-handed. Have you noticed as believers we often feel we need to spiritualize *everything*? It reminds me of the Sunday school class where the teacher called on a young boy, and asked, "Tommy, what is grey, climbs trees, eats nuts and has a large bushy tail?"

Little Tommy sighed and said, "Well, I know the answer is Jesus – but it sure sounds like a squirrel to me!"

If you can glean anything spiritual or practical from this, be my guest. Kenny and I agree the only person who managed to benefit from the whole debacle was me…and all I got was a chapter for a book. Oh, and thirty-three cents.

A man lost his hair. He said, "I now have only a beach where the waves used to be."

12

LAUREN

She was small for her age – not quite three feet tall – and she looked way up at the bank tellers and politely asked what they were doing. They explained to her, in language that a three-year-old would understand, what tellers do.

After their explanation, she replied, "Well, let me ask you another question. Do you find your job rewarding?"

The bank tellers still talk about the incident. I know because it's where I do my banking. And the little girl? She's my daughter.

If Dennis the Menace and Shirley Temple married and had a child, she would be just like our Lauren. My wife, Melanie, claims Lauren is three little boys wrapped up in a little girl's body. She is completely at home playing in a dirt pile with a frog in each hand or in a pretty dress singing up on stage in front of an audience. No one meets Lauren and forgets her. Some people have the personality of a clenched fist. Then there are those like Lauren: bright, bubbly, relishing every moment of any situation. I have never in all my life met anyone more alive. When Lauren exits a room, she leaves a wake.

Make no mistake – she is fun but also fiercely independent. Lauren is the poster girl for the strong-willed child. We jokingly said a good website address for her would be www. getdownfromthere. com. There is no way to share all our Laurenisms in a single chapter, but if you will please allow me, I want to introduce you to our pride and joy.

When Melanie and I married, I actually got two for the price of one. Melanie had Lauren from a previous marriage. Lauren was 2 years old when we married. After the wedding they moved in, and I was amazed at the energy a toddler possesses. After the first couple of hours of witnessing this demonstration of perpetual motion, I thought, *This has been fun. Can we just take the batteries out, put her up on a shelf and get her down another day?*

I quickly learned it doesn't work that way. I found out that Lauren only operated on two settings – on or off – and just two speeds – full throttle or total collapse. She was wide open and into everything, and always giving 100%, but this was brand new to me. Those of you with tiny tykes know exactly what I'm talking about. Whether it's a jaw-dropping, wide-eyed enthusiastic response to a butterfly sighting or the gusto in eating a simple meal, with food flying in every direction – in the floor, on her face, in her hair – it's all or none. Have you noticed when preschoolers get tickled they laugh all over themselves? When they throw a fit, it's "Katie bar the door 'cause they're not taking any prisoners." No matter where they are when they throw a fit – if it's in the grocery store or church aisle – it's a doozy.

Those of you with little ones know how sincerely they live their lives. There's not a fake bone in their little bodies. I just hoped I would be on the right side of the learning curve. After being a bachelor for so many years, I suddenly found myself a husband and a father on the same day. As a microwave dad, I had – and have – lots to learn.

Lauren and I became fast friends. We had an instant rapport. On her own, she started calling me "Daddy." I'm convinced there is not a sweeter sound than to hear the word "Daddy" spoken from the lips of a little one. "Hold me, Daddy, I'm cold." "Hug me, Daddy, I'm scared." All the demands and stresses of the workplace dissolve when you hear that wonderful moniker spoken with a slight baby lisp. Is there a sweeter sound than to hear, "Daddy's home! Daddy's home!"? I never would have guessed so much pure love could be packaged so small, and I never dreamed you could have so much love for someone so tiny. Hot tears have made more than one slalom run down the ski slopes of my cheeks when I realized how undeserving I am to share in the love of this child.

I'm not trying to win a "Dad of the Year" contest, but it has been a high priority for me to make time to do things together with Lauren. We try to build things, read books, tell stories, go on daddy and daughter dates, etc. Lauren and I have fished and flown airplanes, we've wrestled in the floor and laughed 'till we cried. We've put diapers on our heads and danced together (long story). I once let her cut my hair with real scissors (an even longer story). I never knew how much fun these little people could be. As a parent you get a marvelous front row seat to rediscover the simple joys of life. What a thrill to view life from a child's eyes. Children truly are gifts from God.

I used to come home for lunch everyday. This was the highlight of my day because of the fun Lauren and I would have. Melanie explained to me when we got married that they were near completion of "potty training." I wasn't sure what that involved and honestly didn't want to know all of the details. I hate to sound extremely naïve here, but I hadn't been around children much. I had managed to live nearly forty years without using the phrase, "potty trained," in a sentence. In typical man fashion, I'd told Melanie, "Well, fine. Whatever. That's your department."

Well, one day I came home from work at lunch like normal, and Lauren greeted me in her usual fashion. She ran head-long into the plexi-glass storm door with her head, knees and elbows banging the glass all the while yelling at the top of her lungs, "DADDY'S HOME!" As soon as I was inside, Lauren wrapped her entire hand around my finger and declared confidently, "Daddy, I've got something to show you!"

She led me down the hall – I assumed to her room. Her gait was sort of a half skip and half march with her head held high. She exclaimed again, with more confidence, "Have I got something to *show* you!"

I never saw it coming. Like the fella who said, "What duck?" shortly before getting knocked in the head, I never saw it coming. I had absolutely no clue what was about to occur. Instead of taking me to her room she led me into the restroom, pointed down into what looked like a miniature plastic port-a-potty and said emphatically, "Look!"

I was flabbergasted, I was aghast, I was thinking, *This is sick! We're not supposed to be in here doing this, actually studying this mess! This is nasty, it's disgusting!*

My knee-jerk reaction was to snatch her up quickly, leave the room and explain to her how you don't gather a crowd and examine this horrible site. (If only we could explain that to the National Endowment for the Arts.)But she interrupted my panic attack by looking up with her eyes as big as saucers and her sweet innocent face that seemed to be asking for approval. Her gaze said, "Tell me I did good, Daddy."

Now here's a dilemma. How do you handle that? I'm a morning radio broadcaster; I get paid to think quick on my feet. I get paid to talk, but I was speechless. There should be some sort of a parenting manual for moments like this—

especially for microwave Dads, who haven't been on the job long. Dr. Dobson, help!

Lauren pointed at the potty, looked up again asking with those big bright eyes, "Tell me, Daddy. Tell me I did good."

I don't mean to be tacky here, but what *do* you say? "Nice color! Great shape!" I dunno, I was at a total loss. I'm not sure what I eventually said. Who knows? But please pray for *all* parents – we're in way over our heads.

Not only does she live life at full throttle, but Lauren is also a very smart little girl. Oh, I know everyone is supposed to think their children and grandchildren are the cutest and brightest, but Lauren is *really* sharp – which complicates things when you're trying to match wits. More often than not, after people meet Lauren, they exclaim, "Do you know how bright your child is? Have you considered having her IQ tested?" Okay, I'm bragging too much, but you would think less of me as a parent if I didn't brag, wouldn't you?

Once, when Lauren was two years old, we were rough-housing, and I accidentally knocked an antique vase over and it shattered. Lauren looked at me and said, "Daddy, this is a terrible situation." Terrible situation? Mighty big words for such an itty-bitty person.

One day, when she was three, I asked if Lauren and Melanie had been swimming that day. She answered, "Sporadically." I'm not making this up. We employed a high school girl to baby-sit Lauren and she nearly wanted us to sign an affidavit, to swear she was only three years old. The babysitter claims that, immediately after we left the house, Lauren plopped down beside her on the couch and said, "So, tell me all about yourself." Lauren then asked about her college plans and asked what she planned to major in. We don't coach her to ask those questions!

Okay, I'm sorry about this is incessant boasting. It's probably sickening by now, but I just wanted you to know I'm a proud papa and our little Lauren is no ordinary child. She is sweet, she is articulate and she loves Jesus. Just be thankful I don't have you cornered, because then I would have to pull out the pictures to show you, too.

Our loveable little learner keeps life exciting for us, that's for certain. My mother-in-law, Kandi Anderson, a columnist for *The Gulf Coast Sun Herald* (the real writer in the family), recalled a Lauren incident.

> If you think your kids are smarter than every one else's, just wait until the grandkid arrives on the scene. There is just no end to their intelligence and insight. I stand amazed at the age-old wisdom that comes from those who have just barely broken out of diapers. Maybe children are the definition of "God uses the foolish things to confound the wise" or it could be that kids are just one step ahead of the adults who think they are in charge. My granddaughter, Lauren, fits the bill on all counts. Grandparents understand this concept, parents struggle with the truth.
>
> Lauren's dad, J. J., was just beginning to grasp the concept of toddler theology when Lauren was three years old. He was also in the process of gaining insight to the time proven reality that you never leave a child of this tender age alone for more than a few seconds. Lauren had been gone for more than a few seconds; she had quietly removed herself from adult supervision for several minutes. Dad, noticing the unusually quiet

hush in the home, quickly began reconnaissance maneuvers only to discover his precious little girl had made a mission of her moments alone.

Mr. Clean himself, J. J. walked into the kitchen to find that the normally stark white tile floor had been transformed into a pool of chocolate and serenely sitting in the midst of the dark liquid was the missing imp. Yes, she had a gallon of rapidly melting ice cream centered between her chubby little legs and with a huge serving spoon in hand she was trying to shovel as much into her tiny mouth as she possibly could. It didn't appear that anything was going to distract her from this mission in munching, not even dad's ire. That's right ya'll, Dad was not a happy camper and he proceeded to explain to Lauren that she had messed up more than the floor. He leveled a barrage of questions like, "How in the world did you get that ice cream? Why did you get that ice cream? Who told you that you could get that ice cream?" and finally, "What in the world do you think you are doing with that ice cream?" Head bowed, Lauren never lost focus on the task at hand, she just continued to dig in the ice cream.

I know you have been right there with *that* daddy. Getting no response from little miss piggy, he got historical, reciting a litany of sins that Lauren had committed from the moment they had met. Finally, while J. J. caught his breath before continuing his tirade, Lauren peered up at him. She looked up at him with raccoon eyes, her face a mask of chocolate. She never broke a sweat; nope, she just raised that big ol' spoon and shook it at him and calmly stated, "Daddy, you need to take your burdens to the Lord and lay 'em down! And when you take 'em there, leave 'em there."

J. J., taken aback by the enormity of the words coming from that tiny little body, retaliated with a frustrated, "You don't know what a burden is!"

To which Lauren volleyed with, "Yes I do, Daddy, they are worries and troubles. And you look mighty troubled!"

Oh, my friend, if we could only learn the value of those words. Troubles vanish and burdens fade when gathered up and placed at the feet of the Father. There are days that we find ourselves in messes that aren't near as sweet as a puddle of chocolate and we need help. Won't you stop when faced with the muddles of life and cast all your cares on Him for He cares for you! That is eternal wisdom come down from the ages and the pages of Truth, sometimes spoken from the mouths of babes and brilliant grandchildren!

Because Lauren has brought much joy into my life, saying goodbye before I go on the road is much tougher than I ever imagined. On one trip shortly after we were married, I was unpacking in my hotel room and unbeknownst to Melanie, Lauren had smuggled a baby doll into my suitcase so I "wouldn't get lonely and so I wouldn't forget her."

Don't worry sweetheart, I could *never* forget you. Lauren shows me unconditional love and makes me feel ten feet tall. I try hard to return the favor.

Once during the fall around Halloween we were driving by several homes that had been "rolled." I'm not sure if this is popular anywhere except the South, but occasionally young people will "roll" or "TP" someone, throwing rolls and rolls of toilet tissue into the trees and bushes and back and forth over the house. It's an impressive, somewhat shocking sight to see lots and lots of white streamers fluttering in the wind, making your home look like a one-float entry in your own private parade!

Sometimes rolling a yard is a prank played on a foe, but more often than not it is an honor – a good-natured surprise salute from kids to someone who is very popular and very much admired. (I know, it's strange tradition. I guess that's what happens after you eat too much grits, fried green tomatoes and collard greens.)

When Lauren saw her first yard that had been rolled, she was aghast from all the horrible mess. "No," we tried to explain, "This was the coach's home and his players did this to show respect and love."

We saw more rolled homes later that week. Lauren had the same reaction: "Oh no, what a mess! How terrible."

"No, actually it's the youth leader's home and it was done to honor him and his wife. It's a sign of love," we explained again.

Lauren must have caught on, because the next time we saw a colossal mess where some late night toilet paper bandits had struck, Lauren exclaimed, "Wow, they must *really* be loved."

My early morning ritual before leaving for work is not complete until I slip into Lauren's room and kiss her on the cheek. Because I leave in the wee hours of the morning, I miss being with my little family around the breakfast table.

On one of those same autumn mornings, after kissing Lauren and as I turned to leave, I got an idea. I retrieved some needed supplies from the restroom, tiptoed back into her room and proceeded to "roll" her bedroom! From the bunk bed to the closet door, from the dresser to the lamp, around and around and crisscrossing multiple times. I crawled out and admired this tangled web of tissue. *Spiderman would be proud*, I thought.

I wish I could've been there to see her reaction, but Mel gave me an eyewitness report. Lauren woke up and shrieked in delight, "Mama! Mama! Come quick. Look Mama, my Daddy loves me! He *really* loves me! Wow, look how much I'm loved." She lay in bed with her hands clasped behind her head, eyes wide staring at all of these "blue ribbons" – this magnificent "trophy case" with all of these paper trophies just for her! Lauren wouldn't allow Mom to clean up the mess. For several days, she literally had to crawl through the doorway to enter her room. You know it really doesn't require a lot of time or money to brighten someone's day or to say a simple, "I love you." Sometimes a firm handshake, a pat on the back, a card, a call or a six-pack of Charmin will go a long way.

We added to our family on March 14, 2001. Sadie Morgan was born. Now I'm completely outnumbered by women. Sadie is our wonderful new addition. She is still under warranty. She is heaven-sent and such a blessing. I love my girls; because of them I'm a rich man. Those of you who are daddies to daughters *know* how blessed we are. We are actually praying for more children – we want a quiver full of arrows. I once heard that a mother is a woman who decorates her life with babies. Lord bring 'em on, we want a houseful.

I love my girls. I would gladly lay down my life without

hesitation for them. No one had better ever try to harm my towheads, 'cause for those two I would fight a grizzly with my bare hands. And if that day occurs and you happen to have ringside seats – don't bet on the grizzly!

And to you future suitors who would aspire to one day come callin' on my daughters – I'd better warn you. I wrestled in high school and was a celebrated sand lot boxer. In a weight lifting tournament I once bench-pressed 260 lbs when I only weighed 148 lbs. (I still have the trophy). And I also have a background in Karate, tiretool and Louisville Slugger. Keep that in mind when you fill out the application to date my daughter. Future boyfriend you just remain a gentleman – and you and I will get along just fine.

Diaper spelled backwards is repaid.

13
HOPE

She sat in a chair in the driveway with a large sign hanging around her neck that read, "Tell me I'm significant, tell me that I matter, that I count for something. Please tell me I'm important, that I'm worth something, anything. Give me a reason to go on living."

When you're not sure what you want to be when you grow up, you get to enjoy a lot of selections from the career smorgasbord of life. I'm a licensed pilot, broadcaster, comedian, keynote speaker, journeyman bricklayer, and I once worked six months in a hog processing plant. (Occasionally, I still wake up in a cold sweat with recurring nightmares of that resume´ stain. Speaking of which, students, your parents wanted me to tell you, "STAY IN SCHOOL! Get that degree!") Hopefully, this wide variety of work experience has helped me to better relate to listeners while I'm on-air.

For approximately ten years, I owned a tree service – residential tree and stump removal. The motto of Jasper Tree Service was: "We'll go out on a limb for you."

I was called a tree surgeon, but jokingly referred to myself as more of a tree paramedic. It was hard work that provided a good workout and it was lucrative. It satisfied my occasional need for adrenalin to be 60 or 70 feet up in the top of a pine tree wielding a chainsaw. Plus, it sort of brings out the pioneer in a man – that macho side that likes to get outdoors and work up a sweat. I would normally cut trees in the evenings and on weekends to finance my "radio habit." (Those of you in the ministry or in television, radio or newspaper work understand the need to moonlight!) Most of the work was done on Saturday so I wouldn't leave a lot of debris in people's yards throughout the week. The ideal plan was to bring in a small crew, start early on Saturday and finish before sunset.

There is one job I will never forget. I arrived just after sunrise with the dump truck, chainsaws, ladder, tree-climbing gear and my Vermeer hydraulic stump grinder. The stump grinder had a 40 horsepower Wisconsin motor, and boy you should've seen that baby gobble up a stump. We unloaded the gear and made ready to "hit the ground running." In keeping with my get-the-job-done-on-Saturday policy we tried to work hard, work safe and work fast. The customer, a sweet lady, who appeared to be in her sixties, came out to greet us. Because of the high-flying circus-like chainsaw acrobatics of a monkey, er, man dangling from the tops of trees, a small crowd of neighbors would sometimes gather.

Today was no exception, and as a special bonus the woman set up a folding metal table in the driveway, laden with snacks. Her daughter, perhaps in her 30s, joined her to help at the refreshment table. We worked hard and fast. The chainsaws were howling and the sawdust was flying. We were hot, tired and thirsty, but we were racing the clock. Unless we kept our heads down and worked extra hard, we would wind up leaving a colossal mess until the following Saturday.

Throughout the day, the lady and her daughter would beckon us over to take a break. I sent the helpers, but stayed behind at the task, feeling the time crunch. I remember really wanting to stop, but the need to hurry persisted. Hospitality abounding, my sweet, thoughtful customer even changed the menu, rotating different selections of all types of snacks with a wide selection of cool drinks to choose from. Not wanting to seem ungrateful, I hurried over to the table and gulped down something to quench my thirst. She tried to engage me in conversation and offered food, but I politely excused myself and hustled back to try to finish the job.

I had hoped if we finished with time to spare I could indeed sit and visit with this sweet lady and her daughter. Many Saturdays, people would watch us and linger for a while, but these two were troopers. They had joined us right after daylight and had stayed in the driveway with their table of goodies until the sun disappeared below the horizon.

We finished the job just in the nick of time. We loaded our equipment carefully in the dark. We were exhausted, but we had accomplished our mission.

The next day I received a telephone call that I will never forget. Sometime after we left the job, the daughter…killed herself. I don't know all of the details, and I didn't ask. I'm not sure what was wrong in her life or what led up to her terrible and tragic decision. I do know this, however, that I was with her on the last day of her life and I never saw her need.

Looking back, I realize, it was as if she sat in a chair in the driveway with a large sign hanging around her neck that read, "Tell me I'm significant, tell me that I matter, that I count for something. Please tell me I'm important and that I'm worth something, anything. Give me a reason to go on living." The sign was there – it may have been invisible to the human eye – but it was there. I just hadn't seen it.

Do you want to hear something really sad? I can't even tell you what she looked like. I'm not sure I ever looked into her eyes. I'm sure I said, "Hello," but that's probably it. All day long she was there. All day, from early morning until dark. She must have been contemplating suicide right there in that chair and she was silently screaming from the depths of her being, "Please God, please give me something, anything, a ray of hope, something to even hang a fingernail on."

I'm ashamed I was not discerning or sensitive that day. I felt terrible for the family and prayed for them, I can't imagine their heartache and loss. I've beaten myself up many days and nights with the, "What ifs." You see, ordinarily when someone engages me in conversation I look for a subtle way to witness for Christ. I have been accused many times of being a fanatic or a Jesus freak, because even on a job I try to casually mention something positive about the Lord. Even a simple, "God's given us a pretty day," because I'm convinced that God's word teaches us that born-again believers are to share their faith.

Maybe that's why God put me near that girl for so long on her last day. On a normal day, I would have enjoyed a conversation with the mother and daughter and, hopefully, I would have picked up on her sadness and shared God's love. In her desperate state, a crumb would have worked, some small morsel of God's word to give her hope. God says in Isaiah, "My word does not return void." I have seen this happen on many occasions. You can just mention the name of Jesus and get results. God honors His word and our boldness and obedience to proclaim His love.

But I failed Him on that day, I had *the* answer to whatever problem she was facing. I have Jesus Christ in my life; I have a personal relationship with Him. He gives me the reason to live! I *know* He forgives sin and offers supernatural help to hurting people. Jesus Christ is a life changer. He changed me! I know the peace, hope and joy of the Lord and generally share the good news, but didn't that time. I've asked and received forgiveness for failing Him and her.

Although I don't know what drove her to such a tragic decision, I *know* she had lost hope. You may have heard it said, "We can go many days without food, several days without water, and even moments without oxygen, but we can't survive without hope." God has made mankind sturdy and resilient. We can rebound against seemingly insurmountable odds. We can bounce back from disappointment, trials and tribulations, health concerns, financial set backs, heartaches, even the death of a loved one – if we don't lose hope. Without hope we give up...completely.

I shared this story for two reasons. First, to challenge all of us to be sensitive to those around us who've lost hope. People we're around everyday may be hurting desperately. They don't always show signs of depression and despair. Relatives, co-workers, friends, even church members, maybe on the brink of giving up. Please watch, listen, love and be discerning to those who may have lost hope.

Second, to encourage *you* if you've lost hope. If you are in the middle of a seemingly hopeless situation, it may be hard for you to believe this simple truth: God loves you and has a wonderful plan for your life. Jeremiah 29:11 says, "For I know the plans I have for you," declares the Lord, "Plans to prosper you and not to harm you, plans to give you hope and a future."

Maybe you feel like you're insignificant. Listen, you are not a loser – you are a winner. God loves you and created you in His image. You were fearfully and wonderfully made. There is not another person like you in the universe. God made you unique and because you are such a limited edition, that makes you a masterpiece. God loves you – you are the apple of His eye. He is head-over-heels in love with you. Listen, if God had a wallet, your picture would be in it.

God longs for you to seek Him and to know Him better and to not lose heart. If you seek Jesus, you will discover how kind and compassionate He is and how safe you can be with Him. Jesus said, "Come unto me, all you who are weary and burdened, and I will give you rest. Take my yoke upon you and learn from me, for I am gentle and humble in heart, and you will find rest for your souls. For my yoke is easy and my burden is light," (Matt 11: 28-30).

He doesn't promise us a life free from pain, but He promises the forgiveness of our sin and the freedom to live and grow and have victory in Him. Trust the lord – please don't give up. Perhaps you think your situation is too hopeless or too overwhelming. Jesus said, "With God all things are possible." All things. Resurrection power is available to you. Miracles, healing, deliverance – it is all possible because of the virgin birth, sinless life, crucifixion and resurrection of Jesus Christ.

Maybe you think no one cares and no one understands what you're going through. There is One who cares and completely understands. Hebrews 4:15-16 says, "For we do not have a high priest who is unable to sympathize with our weaknesses, but we have one who has been tempted in every way, just as we are – yet was without sin. Let us then approach the throne of grace with confidence, so that we may receive mercy and find grace to help us in our time of need." Jesus was betrayed, misunderstood, abandoned and tortured. He went through every cruel and terrible thing imaginable. That is why He not only has sympathy, but empathy. You can cast all of your cares on Him because He cares for you.

Please, before you give up completely, give Jesus a chance. He is faithful, patient, loving and kind. He will receive you in all your brokenness. He will take you just as you are. Right now, if you are in a depressed, hopeless state, cry out to God in Jesus Name for help. Help is on the way! You're going to make it. Don't quit, don't stop, don't give up or give in, don't throw in the towel. There is hope and help in Jesus.

Therefore, since we have been justified through faith, we have peace with God through our Lord Jesus Christ, through whom we have gained access by faith into this grace in which we now stand. And we rejoice in the hope of the glory of God. Not only so, but we also rejoice in our sufferings, because we know that suffering produces perseverance; perseverance, character; and character, hope. And hope does not disappoint us, because God has poured out his love into our hearts by the Holy Spirit, whom he has given us (Romans 5: 1-5).

Against all hope, Abraham in hope believed and so became the father of many nations, just as it had been said to him, 'So shall your offspring be.' Without weakening in his faith, he faced the fact that his body was as good as dead – since he was about a hundred years old – and that Sarah's womb was also dead. Yet he did not waver through unbelief regarding the promise of God, but was strengthened in his faith and gave glory to God, being fully persuaded that God had power to do what he had promised. This is why "it was credited to him as righteousness," (Romans 4:18-22).

May the God of hope fill you with all joy and peace as you trust in him, so that you may overflow with hope by the power of the Holy Spirit (Romans 5:13).

———•••——

Triumph is just "umph" added to try.

———•••——

14
THE SHACK

Dorothy, Karen and some other girls from church would occasionally volunteer to clean the place. The house was 100 years old, huge and rickety. Because of its condition, the girls called it "The Shack," and the nickname stuck.

The whole experience began one Saturday in the late '70s, when I found myself apartment hunting in Owensboro, Kentucky. I ran into my cousin, Kevin, who with the "classifieds" in hand, was doing exactly the same thing.

Kevin's mom and my dad were brother and sister, but since he was nearer in age to my younger sisters, we hadn't been especially close. However, we had grown closer after he dedicated his life to Christ. At the time I thought bumping into Kevin was merely a coincidence.

After lamenting the lack of affordable places to rent, Kevin offered a suggestion. Our grandmother's house was vacant, and he felt sure we could move in there. So we drove to the busy corner of 18th and Alexander Streets on the east end of town and looked the place over.

The weeds and overgrown bushes testified to how long it had been since our grandmother, Hettie Jasper-Dause, had been laid to rest. The old white clapboard siding was faded and peeling. Our grandmother raised seven children in that house, including Kevin's mom and my dad, and this big old house, sprawled out on this corner lot, was truly on its last leg.

After a cursory walk through we immediately agreed that it was at least worth a try. First, however, we decided to kneel down in prayer and dedicate the home to the Lord. I remember our fervent, earnest prayer on bended knees with outstretched arms, as we asked God to bless this venture and to use this old place for His glory.

I said at first I thought that crossing paths with Kevin had been a coincidence. I later changed my mind. As it turned out, two cousins who just *happened* to meet up while apartment hunting – never having even considered the possibility of ever becoming roommates – were about to embark on something completely life-changing.

When we knelt to pray in that old run down, abandoned house, we had no idea that God was about to do something mighty and magnificent. In fact, what followed was a monumental chapter in my life that would require an entire book to properly tell the story. The impact and significance of those days can't compare with any other events in my entire life.

When Kevin and I prayed, we'd ask God to use Grandma's house for His glory. Like the old saying goes, "You should be careful what you pray for." Only several days had passed when our pastor learned of a young boy who was in jail on a minor charge and could be released only under two conditions. First, he had to have a job, and second, he had to have a place to live.

Someone had already provided, a job, but with no family in the area he had nowhere to go. Our pastor asked us if the young man could bunk with us for a while until he got on his feet.

We agreed, and that was the first of *many* runaways, hitchhikers and recovering alcoholics and drug addicts who came to room with us. Without ever intending to do so, Kevin and I found ourselves running a full-fledged halfway house.

Kevin and I were the entire staff for the first five months. At one point, the inmates were running the asylum, and we were outnumbered significantly. Kevin got married and moved away during the early boot camp stages. After he left, other committed "on fire for the Lord" young men came on board and the ratio between the lions and the lion tamers began to balance out. Regretfully, "Warden Kevin" never really got to see the entire operation get up and running smoothly before he left.

We wound up with approximately seven full-time, live-in volunteer youth workers, and a revolving door of short-term visitors who would stay weeks or months until they were up on their feet and able to move on. Again, although we hadn't planned it this way, we had a full-scale ministry that was like David Wilkerson's "Teen Challenge."

Picture, if you can, our unique lifestyle. There were seven to ten young men living together, and since each of us had at least *one* friend, we had a houseful each evening. Can you imagine? Every night we had over a dozen people at our home!

On Tuesday nights I led a Bible study, which drew about 50 young people. Everyone crammed into the living room as best they could, sitting cross-legged on the floor, all over the couches, on *top* of the old upright piano, spilling over into the dining room – everywhere. After a time, a local church graciously paid the rent on a commercial building in a shopping mall so we could hold the Tuesday night meetings there.

Surprisingly, with so many folks at "The Shack" each night, there was order, not chaos, and there was a sweet spirit and sweet peace.

We had cookouts in the vacant lot beside our old house with turnouts that bordered on spring break proportions. We would have 100 or more young people in their teens and in their twenties, having all of the drug and alcohol-free fun you could stand. We tossed Frisbees and played endless hours of horseshoes and volleyball.

Many of us had been used to going to clubs, bars and hangouts when we lived a different lifestyle, so after our conversion, we sometimes felt isolated and alone. There didn't seem to be a place in the community where Christians could go – a place where "everyone knows your name." It's a long stretch between Sundays or from Sunday to Wednesday – especially when you were used to getting off work and stopping by a friendly place with familiar faces to unwind or share your day with someone who cares.

"The Shack" seemed to fill that niche and provide a Christian hangout – sort of an oasis for the soul. When someone successfully shared their faith with a co-worker or had an answer to prayer and couldn't wait to tell someone – we were there. They didn't have to wait until Sunday morning, because they felt free to stop by after work while they were still enthused and excited and it was fresh. If they had a bad day or a great day, or if they just needed some fellowship, we were on call 24 hours a day. I've wondered if perhaps a lot of those new Christians might have lost interest without a place to ask questions or share an enthusiastic testimony of a recent victory in their Christian walk.

There always seemed to be plenty of activity going on around the clock at "The Shack." We all worked different jobs with varied shifts. The house had lots of rooms and on any given day someone might be playing the guitar in one room while several were studying their Bibles in another. Other guys would be counseling or praying with someone elsewhere, while someone else would be lying in the floor in another room, listening to the stereo with headphones on.

We had lots of rooms, but, oddly, we only used one large room for a bedroom. *One* bedroom! We had three racks of bunk beds and the rest of the bedroom was covered with twin beds.

We had totally dedicated our entire lives to Him – and He did not disappoint us. When Almighty God, the maker of the universe, comes over to your house to pay you a celestial visit amazing things happen! The events that transpired at "The Shack" were almost like reading from the pages of the Bible. We were actually *living* New Testament Christianity, and New Testament things began to happen.

We routinely – yes, I am aware of the word I chose here – we *routinely* saw people delivered from the bondage of drugs and alcohol addiction. We saw people set free from the destructive homosexual lifestyle. Many times we saw young people rescued from suicidal tendencies. We witnessed people healed, and saw literal miracles. And we often saw the greatest miracle of all – Salvation! Young people came to realize their need for God, repented of their sins and received Jesus Christ into their hearts and lives by faith.

We had jail ministries, street ministries, we went to discos and dances and sat in the parking lot on the tailgate of our pick-up truck where talented musicians would play the guitar and sing. As a crowd would gather we would share the good news and hand out gospel tracts.

We looked for opportunities to reach people, especially the neglected and the down-and-outers. You would be surprised how many lonely people you'll find in a laundromat who just need a new friend, someone who will care and just listen. We loved Jesus with all our hearts and we "hung out a shingle" that let hurting people know that Jesus loved them and so did we. Folks were drawn to "The Shack" in droves.

All this may seem unbelievable or hard to understand or perhaps it doesn't gel with your theology, but I feel compelled to share these facts because, as an eyewitness, I was there. These things actually happened! There is a lot I can't explain and much I don't understand, but this much I do know: if you are there and you see it happen – it makes a believer out of you.

Churches from many different denominations all across town heard of our reputation and called us with their "hopeless cases." We received runways, addicts and homeless people from all over. We eventually got referrals from schools as well as city and county agencies.

I was surprised and a little concerned that there wasn't an agency or program in place to handle those who were desperate. We got 'em all. And the God of the universe who specializes in tough cases came on the scene over and over again, working mightily through His precious Holy Spirit. I can't explain it all, but as we served the Lord at "The Shack," we witnessed documented episodes of healing, deliverance and salvation.

Keep in mind we had no program and no budget. We didn't have a five-minute plan – much less a five-year strategic plan. We had no committees, and I can't remember a single staff meeting. We didn't consult the home office to sign off on our efforts. We weren't board certified or seminary trained, and we had no "official" qualifications to counsel people.

We were unlearned and ignorant men who had been

with Jesus. Our approach was simple, we relied on God's word and our method was Jesus – plus nothing. To some people, it may all seem unorthodox and naïve, but we got results! I could fill these pages with names and stories of former drug users, prostitutes and convicts who became clean, happily married people who served their local churches and made a contribution as model citizens.

One evening a deputy sheriff knocked on the door of "The Shack." He asked to speak with whoever was in charge. They came and got me, and I thought, *Oh, no, I'll bet it's another parking violation.* With limited parking spaces our friends parked everywhere, up and down the street.

The deputy asked to speak with me in private. He explained that although he was not "right with God," at one time he had been. The officer explained that he had responded to a call to the ministry and even pastored a church at one time. He went on to explain that although he wasn't where he should be spiritually, he wanted to help us at "The Shack." He had been watching us and had us checked out. He confirmed that we were legitimate.

"Off the record," he said, "I want to make you a proposal. At my discretion, I want to offer someone a choice to either go to jail or spend the night with your group and hear the gospel."

He went on to explain that many weekends he picked up *good* kids who were drinking or doing some other kind of first-time offense. "I hate to see a kid go to jail and get a criminal record, to be marked by that for life and ruin many future opportunities," he said. "I know some of these kids don't need to spend a night in jail – they need Jesus in their lives."

We prayed about it, talked it over and agreed to the deputy's proposal. And that meant that our weekends just got busier. When the blue lights appeared in their rearview mirror, and after being given a choice either to go to jail or to hear preaching, which do you suppose those frightened teens selected? Many weekends, we had a steady stream of patrons in the wee hours of the morning. Between pots of black coffee, we saw a lot of young people come to Christ because of that innovative officer's bold plan.

There were many incredible stories of God's faithfulness at "The Shack." One time two insurance salesmen knocked on our door to do some "cold calling." Moments after they came inside, they said they felt something *different* going on. With tears welling up in their eyes they asked, "Who are you guys? What is this place?"

Then one of the men started confessing his sins – we hadn't said one word. I suppose the men sensed the presence of God in that place.

Many times people would show up on our doorstep and say, "I don't know why I'm here. I can't explain it, *something* just told me I needed to stop here!" This happened with such frequency, we didn't even consider it bizarre.

On another occasion, we had gone across the street to the corner grocery to buy food. We were in the store getting meat, and the elderly butcher was processing our order. After some small talk, he mentioned that he was scheduled for serious surgery in a few days and had some very real concerns. We shared a brief testimony of God's love, power and ability to heal. We asked permission to pray for him.

Well, the short version of the story is this: after being prepped for surgery the doctors ordered one last set of X-rays, and upon examining them – the man was cured! There was no need for surgery. The doctors offered no medical explanation.

Of course, we were convinced it was an answer to prayer. Later, when our neighbors would be in the store and the

gossip turned to comments about those freaks c
across the street, the butcher would defend us. .
boldly say, "You'd better lay-off those boys – they're g
kids, they're right with God, and they're my new best
friends."

The butcher would share his healing testimony with
people and explain that he could give out his doctors' names
and point to the X-rays if there were any doubters. Wouldn't
you know it, that butcher became a one-man public rela-
tions firm for "The Shack!" Our approval rating in the community soared. Not only that, but he started collecting
prayer requests from customers and every week, when we
would go to the store, he would present us with a long list
of prayer needs. Isn't God good!

Looking back, I wonder why we experienced such a
mighty outpouring of God's Holy Spirit during that season at "The Shack." I now see some patterns and understand that though we didn't realize it, we had positioned
ourselves for a glorious visit from God. The atmosphere at
"The Shack" was conducive for revival. Please allow me to
try and explain.

Not unlike the first church, we were in one accord. We
were a small bunch of saved by grace young people who
humbled themselves and were focused on simply glorify-
ing God in all of our words and deeds, even capturing
thoughts to bring them in submission to Christ's Lord-
ship. We strived to love the Lord with our whole mind,
soul, body and strength and love our neighbors as ourselves. Our mission all day and every day was to win people
to Him.

We were unselfishly sold out. We worked at different
jobs, put all our money in a pot, paid bills and bought
food, then used our own money to buy food, clothes and

Bibles for the poor. We lived by faith – no one was on salary and we had no funds from outside sources – and God always honors that.

And we weren't *worldly.* I don't expect everyone to understand this, but we purposely owned no television and tried to surround ourselves with godly friends and music. We were zealous to have only pure influences in our lives and it was working. What they say is true: "Garbage in, garbage out." We were uncompromising in the type of movies we went to watch. You would be amazed at how much easier it is to seek God and hear from Him without an avalanche of secular influences bombarding you.

We tried to be dead to ourselves daily and offer empty, clean vessels for Him to use. Our lives are like a container. If we fill our lives up with all of our selfish wants and desires continually, we leave no room for Jesus – and you have a shallow existence. If we empty our lives of selfish ambition and daily take up our cross and follow Jesus, He will fill us – gloriously fill us! You can have as much of God in your life as you choose. If you are full of yourself, there is little room for God. If we die to self, that leaves room for God to abide in us and assume His rightful place, seated on the throne of our hearts.

We weren't even aware of how many spiritual principles we were triggering. We *studied* God's word. There *is* a difference between just reading and *studying.* The Bible instructs us to study to show ourselves approved, a workman that need not be ashamed.

Someone was *always* reading God's word and someone was *always* praying. I've never been in an environment that was more bathed in God's word, prayer and praise.

We fasted and prayed – and I mean we *really* prayed! The old timers call it laying hold of the horns of the altar.

We travailed in prayer. We would sit cross-legged in a circle on the floor and sometimes pray for *several* hours. Nowadays it seems that after I pray for several minutes, my mind starts to wander and I get off track. But back then we would pray and continue praying past the point when you're restless and bored, pressing in and truly crying out to Almighty God for unsaved loved ones and petitioning God to deliver friends who were trapped in life-controlling sins.

There is a point in *serious* prayer where you break through, you enter in. It's hard to explain in words, and I wonder, in our fast-paced culture, how many Christians have ever prayed for *hours.* Jesus spoke of victory in desperate situations through prayer and fasting.

You can reach a deeper place in God, but it requires sacrifice. The prerequisite is to hunger and thirst. No, it's not based on works, and it isn't based in legalism. It is earnestly reaching out to God in faith in the name of Jesus.

The spirit is willing but the flesh is weak, yet God rewards spiritual diligence. Hebrews 11:6 (KJV) says, "He who comes to God must believe that He *is,* and that He is a rewarder of them who diligently seek Him." Throughout the Bible, there is an invitation from God to seek Him with all your heart, to hunger and thirst for righteousness. And the promise is that you shall be filled!

Victory, spiritual break-throughs and revival don't happen by accident. We won't just drift and find ourselves in the center of God's will. I found out living at "The Shack" that you can have as much of God as you want, but you have to be willing to pay the price.

God is not our butler or an old buddy. He is the omnipresent, omnipotent God who created heaven and earth. It is a fearful thing to fall into the hands of the living God, but thankfully He's given us the privilege through Jesus

Christ to enter into the Holy of Holies and boldly ask for help in our time of need.

For the most part this book has been lighthearted. My desire was to encourage you through humorous stories and anecdotes. When I began reflecting on "The Shack," however, I felt that a different tone was needed. But as the proverbial "class clown" and cut-up, I knew I was running a risk that people would not take me seriously when it came to talking about "The Shack." Let me assure you – there is no punch line to this story.

As honestly and sincerely as I can, I've attempted to describe a chapter in my life where God took a handful of ordinary young men and paid us a visit from on high that resembled experiences from the Book of Acts.

No season in my life has ever come close to rivaling how we saw God move in that old house. I'll never forget that Christian "Green Beret," in-the-trenches type of ministry, shoulder-to-shoulder with Kevin, Rex, James, David, Johnny, Jimmy, Mark, Greg, Dwayne, Tommy, Lyndal, Garbonzo and all the others.

This is a simple, eyewitness account of God's glory. It happened. I was there. And so were hundreds of others who witnessed the mighty miracles that took place at the corner of 18th and Alexander Streets.

For 20 years I've pondered the wonderful experiences we shared at "The Shack." Maybe someday the Lord will lead me to write a book about those days, as a testimony of God's incredible love and faithfulness. For now, a chapter will have to do. I hope it will inspire you to write a chapter of your own.

———•••••———

Do you know Jesus? Having a personal relationship with Jesus Christ is more than just being religious or even being a church member. Do you *know* Him? Jesus said, "I am the way and the truth and the life. No one comes to the Father except through me," (John 14:6).

One day, I realized my need for God, humbled myself, repented of my sins and received Jesus Christ into my heart and life by faith. It was the greatest decision I have ever made.

Is there a void in your life? Are you unfulfilled? Does your life seem hollow and frustrating? I have good news. Jesus Christ is a life-changer!

God loves you and has a wonderful plan for your life, but sin separates us from God. Because God loves us so much, He made a way for us. When Jesus died on the cross, He took on Himself our own punishment for all we have ever done wrong. He canceled our debt to sin. We're no longer separated from a perfect God because of our sin. When we believe in Jesus, we're forgiven for all our sins, once and for all. We can have peace and joy that comes from knowing that God loves us and forgives us. The Bible says in John 3:16, "For God so loved the world that He gave His one and only Son, that whoever believes in Him shall not perish, but have eternal life.

Ephesians 2:8-9 (KJV) says, "For by grace are ye saved through faith; and that not of yourselves: it is the gift of God: Not of works, lest any man should boast." Salvation is a gift. Would you like to have a right relationship with Almighty God? All you have to do is ask. It's really simple:

• **Admit** to Him that you have done wrong, that you have sinned.

• **Ask** God to forgive you of all your sins

• **Believe** that Jesus died for your sins on a cross and was raised from the dead.

• **Choose** to follow Him.

Do you want to receive this free gift God promises to give you? You can ask right now by praying this prayer:

Dear God,

I admit that I am a sinner, and I know that my sin separates me from you. I believe that Jesus took my punishment for all my sins by dying on the cross and being raised from the dead. Thank you for loving me. Please forgive me of all my sins. Please come into my heart and life. Thank you for forgiving me. Thank you for giving me the gift of eternal life. Help me to learn more about you and grow to be more like you.

In Jesus' name I pray, Amen.

If you were sincere and prayed this prayer from your heart, you have now become a child of God, through faith in Jesus Christ. Congratulations!

Contact a local pastor and let them know of your decision or please contact 1-800-NEED HIM for more information.

American Family Filter

As a man I understand and have experienced the temptation of pornography. The popularity of computers and the increased traffic on the Internet have brought many benefits, but offered dangerous pitfalls.

As a husband and father I strive to protect myself and my family from harmful influences. That's why we have the American Family Filter on our home computer. I personally recommend it to you.

The American Family Filter is a Christian Internet filter for the whole family!

The benefits of having a strong filter, like the American Family Filter, for your children are obvious. There is a wealth of great information and educational tools on the Internet, but the real fear of being victimized by pornography, chat rooms, and other offensive and objectionable content has kept many families away from this valuable medium.

The American Family Filter is a server based filter. This means blocking objectionable sites before they reach your computer. The block list is updated daily, resulting in higher accuracy and no confusing database updates for you to download or worry about. The American Family Filter has no password overrides. This means no guessed or cracked passwords, resulting in better security and protection for your whole family.

Our family is very satisfied with the protection we receive from American Family Filter and we whole-heartedly recommend it to you.

For more information, go to www.afafilter.com.

To order additional copies or
to correspond please contact:

JJJasper
P.O. Box 804
Tupelo, MS 38802

or visit

www.JJJasper.com